T0206293

Artificial Intelligence in Medical Imaging

Artificial Intelligence in Medical Imaging

From Theory to Clinical Practice

Lia Morra
Silvia Delsanto
Loredana Correale

CRC Press is an imprint of the
Taylor & Francis Group, an **informa** business

CRC Press
Taylor & Francis Group
6000 Broken Sound Parkway NW, Suite 300
Boca Raton, FL 33487-2742

First issued in paperback 2021

ISBN-13: 978-0-367-22917-7 (hbk)
ISBN-13: 978-1-03-217646-8 (pbk)
DOI: 10.1201/9780367229184

This book contains information obtained from authentic and highly regarded sources. Reasonable efforts have been made to publish reliable data and information, but the author and publisher cannot assume responsibility for the validity of all materials or the consequences of their use. The authors and publishers have attempted to trace the copyright holders of all material reproduced in this publication and apologize to copyright holders if permission to publish in this form has not been obtained. If any copyright material has not been acknowledged please write and let us know so we may rectify in any future reprint.

Trademark Notice: Product or corporate names may be trademarks or registered trademarks, and are used only for identification and explanation without intent to infringe.

Publisher's Note

The publisher has gone to great lengths to ensure the quality of this reprint but points out that some imperfections in the original copies may be apparent

**Visit the Taylor & Francis Web site at
http://www.taylorandfrancis.com**

**and the CRC Press Web site at
http://www.crcpress.com**

To our families.

Contents

Preface

The notion of artificial intelligence is closely tied to the birth of the first computing systems, although references to thought-capable artificial beings are present in earlier times of human history. Early references emerge searching far into the past as in ancient Greece, where mythological tales described robots with human-like appearance created by the god Hephaestos, or in China, where thought-capable machines were represented [1].

The foundation of most of the current developments in artificial intelligence may be placed in the study of formal logic, developed by Aristotle in the western world, and in parallel elsewhere, as in India and in China. In 1936, Alan Turing developed on these concepts his theory of computation, which suggested that mathematical deductions could be performed by a machine by using binary symbols. Turing also formulated the famous words: "I propose to consider the question, 'Can machines think?'" and devised the best-known test to determine the "intelligence" of a machine, when he stated that if a human observer is incapable of distinguishing the response of a machine from that of a human, then the machine may be described as able to think. Anecdotal occasions in which competing machines at events fooled part of the jury have been reported in the last years [2], and in a recent demo at Google I/O 2018, Google's digital assistant demonstrated the capability to accomplish tasks such as reserving a dinner table at a restaurant in a manner virtually indistinguishable from that of a human being.

An interesting aspect in the definition of artificial intelligence is that the very concept evolves rapidly in time, as machine capacity of performing tasks grows, in what has been dubbed as the AI Effect. Tasks which a few years back were eminently considered as part of artificial intelligence such as optical character recognition are taken for granted as additional functionalities of computer systems, while researchers and philosophers at the frontiers of technology are starting to consider the possibility of capabilities far beyond what humans can achieve today, in a future where AI systems reach omniscience and technological growth becomes exponential and uncontrollable, with unpredictable consequences on human life.

In practice, artificial intelligence systems today are generally oriented to very specific tasks and typically assist human activity, rather than altogether replace it. These feats are mostly accomplished through Machine Learning, the form of AI which we focus on in this book and which we will introduce in Chapter 1.

The perspective however is starting to change with the advent of deep learning, as the performance of AI systems is dramatically improving and reaching a level comparable to that of experts on complex tasks, as we will see in many examples throughout the book. Deep learning neural networks are a particular form of Machine Learning, enabled by recent advancements in computational power and data availability, which are characterized by a greater complexity and a higher level of automation. We will describe the foundation of these techniques in Chapter 2. In Chapter 3, we will describe how these methodologies have been applied in Medical Imaging, starting from the first applications, in which the image processing component was prevalent, on to the systems capable of providing a standalone evaluation of clinical cases which we are starting to see today. Finally, in Chapter 4 we offer an overview of the complexity of clinical evaluation for AI systems to be used on a real patient population and describe how continuously learning systems create challenges for the regulatory framework.

CHAPTER 1

Fundamentals of Machine Learning

O ne of the most common processes by which computing systems achieve the capability to perform sophisticated tasks
is called machine learning, and it essentially consists in learning
by examples, much as we human beings do. This route, which may
at first seem obvious, was not the mainstream approach in early
AI systems, which were more often based on the definition and
application of rules. This was mostly due to the fact that learning by examples requires both data and computational power to
be successful. Rules however do present many exceptions, as our
experience tells us, and that is one of the reasons early so-called
expert systems failed and created a wave of disillusionment on AI
capabilities.

To understand how machine learning is implemented, it is useful to consider how we humans learn and perform tasks ourselves.
If we wish to recognize a plant amongst many, for instance, we will
first look at a lot of examples of plants and perhaps read some
indications on how to distinguish them. We might see for example
that the stem is long, and that the leaves are wide and of a certain
color and that the veins are specifically oriented. Here we are implicitly doing different elementary tasks. We are in the first place
perceiving the images or the examples with our eyes. In medical
imaging, the analogous of sight is image acquisition. Then, we are
recognizing that a certain part of the plant is the stem and another
is the leaf. This is what in image processing is called image segmentation. In medical imaging applications, this may mean identifying

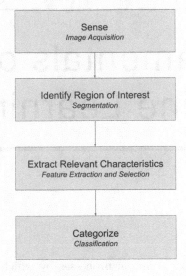

Figure 1.1 Steps of a machine learning classification process.

which part of a mammographical image is chest muscle or identifying grey and white matter in brain MRI scans. Segmentation may be a necessary step for feature extraction, but is also has important applications in its own right, as we will see in the following.

Going back to our example, we are also considering that the length of the stem and the color of leaf are important features for discrimination. If we are lucky, we may already know which features are relevant, but in other cases we may need to look at many different examples in order to identify which features may help to distinguish our plant. We are now mentioning a few very high level features, but in practice we often have dozens or hundreds of possible measures which be may very detailed and related to each other, such as the length of primary and secondary veins in the leaf. The process of identifying and selecting the most discriminant features is called feature selection and extraction. Finally, we have to combine and relatively weigh the information given by these features to decide whether the plant we are looking at is an eggplant or a tomato. This is the classification step.

Our botanical example describes the fundamental steps of classical machine learning techniques, synthetized in Figure 1.1. The description "classical machine learning" has recently originated in consequence to the increasing growth of a new branch of machine learning, deep learning, which has demonstrated impressive capabilities by enabling feature learning, as will be explored in Chapter 2. In this chapter, we will provide a few key notions for the novice, in order to guide through the concepts that will be developed in various applications throughout the book. The intention here is not to provide a comprehensive overview of classical machine learning, for which more detailed references will be provided, but rather to offer a brief overview of the process, with a few examples.

1.1 FEATURE EXTRACTION AND SELECTION

Feature selection and extraction are key steps in classical machine learning applications. Feature extraction typically refers to the process by which the extraction of characteristics which are useful for classification, or correlation with predicted states or outcomes is performed. Once the features have been extracted, the process of feature selection begins, in which the objective is to optimally reduce the number of variables which are input to the classifier or intended for regression analysis.

1.1.1 Feature Extraction

Feature extraction is particularly important in machine learning imaging applications, as data must be extracted from the images in order to be passed to a classifier. Given the focus of our book we will here concentrate on feature selection for image processing applications.

Features extracted from medical images and indeed from images in general may be divided in three main categories: first order features (intensity or shape based), second order features (texture-based) and higher-order features, which capture image information at different frequencies.

Intensity-based features are summary statistics such as mean, median, standard deviation and higher-order moments such as skewness and kurtosis which capture how intensity levels are varying in a region of interest. In some cases, this may be efficiently performed by operating a convolution of a $N \times N$ kernel with the image, by which a sliding window, performing a matrix multiplication at each step. For example, operating a convolution with a

3×3 kernel with all values equal to 1 corresponds to performing a mean for each pixel in a 3×3 neighbourhood. The choice of the kernel and of the neighbourhood define the image features that are being extracted and it is this choice that is automated through the convolutional networks in deep learning. Other examples of commonly used features based on pixel intensity distribution are entropy, which measures the degree of randomness in the pixel intensity distribution, and uniformity, which are among the most employed features in radiomics [3].

Shape-based features, on the other hand, describe the geometry of the region of interest, which often coincides with the segmentation of suspect lesion candidates and may be an estimation of the volume, height, curvature, shape index, diameter or surface to volume ratio. The evaluation of these features may be rather straightforward, as in the case of volume, or require a preceding specific segmentation step, as in the case of indexes measuring the presence of spicules in mammographic lesions.

Texture features, also called second order radiomics features in the relative applications, aim at describing the nature of intensity heterogeneity in regions of interest by exploring the relation between pixel intensity and space. Texture features are derived from descriptive matrices. Examples of these descriptive matrices may be the gray level co-occurrence matrix (GLCM), which describes the times in which two intensity levels appear in two pixels at a given distance and angle, or the gray level run-length (GLRL), which quantifies the lengths of consecutive pixels having the same intensity.

Finally, higher order features describe image patterns through filters such as in space-frequency analysis methods as the Fourier transform or wavelets or as in fractal analysis.

1.1.2 Feature Selection

Feature selection aims at increasing the tractability of the data by eliminating the less informative ways and may be expressed in two different ways, i.e. as the identification of the combination of features which most compactly represents the drivers of the given problem or the determination of the features which bring the best results to subsequent classification. In any case, the process of feature selection should be robust to transformations in data such as preprocessing, should select the features which bring the information which is more relevant to the classification task and should not include features which are redundant.

In the first declination, the emphasis is on dimensionality reduction based on the intrinsic distribution of the features and as the classification step is not considered and information brought by class labels is not exploited, these techniques are named unsupervised techniques. A classic example of this kind of techniques is Principal Component Analysis (PCA), where a transformation of the original variables is performed with the condition of successively extracting orthogonal components of the maximum possible variance at each step. Another slightly different transformation is Independent Component Analysis (ICA), which transforms variables under the assumption that the observed data are given by an addition of independent non-Gaussian distributed sources.

Supervised methods for feature selection are perhaps the most common way of performing feature selection in medical imaging processing tasks involving classification. A complete taxonomy of supervised feature selection methods is presented in [4]. A first distinction is made between neural network-based techniques based on node pruning and statistical pattern recognition techniques. The latter are then subdivided into optimal techniques, which explore classification performances for all possible feature combinations and suboptimal techniques, which may be based on the refinement of a single solution. For example, in feedforward selection methods, the solution is grown incrementally by selecting at each step the feature which most improves the classification accuracy. On the contrary, evolutionary strategies such as genetic algorithms can test many possible solutions simultaneously. Multivariate supervised feature selection methods are also named wrapper methods, as they are in fact a wrapper step of the classification process itself.

The feature selection step is particularly important in radiomics applications, where often hundreds of different features are extracted, but is as important to other applications as well. In general, it is worth remembering that in order to achieve an initial understanding of the distribution of data, often more simple, univariate approaches can be helpful as a starting point.

For more details, the interested reader is referred to the vast literature describing various techniques for feature extraction; the article by Guyon and Elisseeff [5] is a classical reference and presents a general framework of the principles of feature extraction, while Sklansky [6] describes various techniques applied in image processing applications.

1.2 STATISTICAL CLASSIFIERS

In broader terms, machine learning includes supervised, unsupervised and semi-supervised learning problems. In a supervised learning scenario, a set of input and output pairs are available (i.e., training data) and the task is to learn the relationship between the inputs and their associated outputs. Given a new input, the learned relationship can be used to predict the corresponding output. An example for a supervised learning task is a classification task: given several examples of a set of objects attributes (i.e., features) and the type (i.e., class) of these objects, a supervised approach can be taken to find the relationship (i.e., classification model) between the features and the associated class, which subsequently allows us to predict the object class for a set of features. This is in contrast with unsupervised learning [7], for which only inputs and no corresponding outputs are available. Unsupervised learning aims to model the underlying structure in inputs data. This paradigm is especially useful to analyze whether there are distinguishable groups or clusters present in the data (i.e., clustering). Between supervised and unsupervised learning is semi-supervised learning [8], i.e., learning where an incomplete training set with some (often many) of the target outputs missing is available.

There exists a wide range of different machine learning techniques that deal with each of the learning problem types. In the remainder of this section we will provide background material concerning the most popular learning approaches to building classification models (i.e., classifiers) from an input dataset. The literature on this topic is so extensive that even a superficial overview of all the main approaches goes far beyond the possibilities of this section. The readers can refer to a number of fundamental books on the subjects [9–11].

Before introducing the different approaches to building a classification model, we will briefly summarize the basic concepts, formalisms and notations. The input data for a classification task is a set of N instances (also known as data records or examples). Each instance is characterized as a tuple $(\boldsymbol{x}, y)$, where $\boldsymbol{x} = (x_1, x_2, ..., x_n)$ is a set of n attributes and y is the label that defines the class this instance belongs to. In the following, we use bold symbols such as $\boldsymbol{x}$ to indicate vectors, and x_k to denote their kth component. Although for most machine learning algorithms features have to be real-valued, feature vectors can also contain discrete values. The class label, on the other hand, must be only discrete and the set of all such possible labels is denoted as $y = \{y_1, y_2, \cdots, y_M\}$. Clearly, this notation includes binary classification as a special case $k = 2$.

Mathematically, classification is the task of learning a target function f that maps each feature vector x to one of the predefined class labels y. The target function is also informally called the classification model or classifier. Thus, a classifier is a function f defined in $\mathcal{X} \subseteq \mathcal{R}^n$ with values in $\{y_1, \cdots, y_M\}$. An important consideration in learning the target function from the training data is how well the model generalizes to new data. In this regard, the goal of a classification task is to learn a classifier f that generalizes well beyond training data in the sense of minimizing the risk of incorrect classification with respect to a specific loss function, i.e., a measure of the error $L(y, f(x))$ the learner encounters when predicting $f(x)$ in place of y.

There are different ways of categorizing the classifiers. A possible distinction is between statistical classifiers (e.g., Bayesian, logistic regression, SVMs) or non-statistical-based classifiers (e.g., rule-based expert systems). A classifier can be linear or nonlinear. The mapping function can be parametric or non-parametric. Some frequently used classifiers are described in the following paragraphs.

1.2.1 Bayesian Classifiers

One popular way to infer the correct class of the instance x is to treat both the feature vector x and the class label y as random variables. In this case, the posterior class probabilities $P(y|x)$ for the given instance x are computed; then the instance x is assigned to the class i, for which the $P(y_i|x)$ is maximum [10,12,13]:

$$x \in y_i, \text{ if } P(y_i|x) > P(y_j|x) \ \forall \ i \neq j \tag{1.1}$$

Despite its simplicity, we do not know the form of $P(y|x)$, but are given a set of N instances $\{(x_i, y_i)\}_{i=1}^{N}$. It is from these prototype instances that we try to estimate $P(y|x)$. According to basic probabilistic rules,

$$P(y_i|x)P(x) = P(y_i, x) = P(x|y_i)P(y_i) \tag{1.2}$$

These rules allow us to estimate $P(y_j|x)$ in terms of $P(x|y_j)$ and $P(y_j)$:

$$P(y_i|x) = \frac{P(x|y_i)P(y_i)}{P(x)} \tag{1.3}$$

whereby we assume that there is a better chance to estimate $P(\boldsymbol{x}|y)$ and $P(y)$ than estimating $P(y|\boldsymbol{x})$ directly. In the denominator, $P(\boldsymbol{x}) = \sum_{i=1}^{M} P(\boldsymbol{x}|y_i)$ is an ignorable normalization constant that ensures the posterior adds up to 1.

In the Bayesian statistics framework, $P(y_i)$ is referred to as the class prior probability, which is the probability that a member of class y_i will occur. This term can be estimated directly from the proportion of class y_i instances in the training set. The function $P(\boldsymbol{x}|y_i)$ is called the class-conditional probability density function, i.e. the probability density of observing instance $\boldsymbol{x}$ given that $\boldsymbol{x}$ is a member of class y_i.

Accurately estimating $P(\boldsymbol{x}|y)$ is however not straightforward, since it involves the estimation of exponential numbers of joint-probabilities of the features. For example, when y is boolean and $\boldsymbol{x}$ is a vector of n boolean features, we need to estimate a set of parameters:

$$\theta_{ki} = P(x_k|y_j)$$

where the index k takes on 2^n possible values (one for each of the possible vector values of x_k), and i takes on 2 possible values. Therefore, we must estimate a total of $2(2^n - 1)$ parameters to characterize $P(\boldsymbol{x}|y)$. Worse yet, to obtain reliable estimates of each of these parameters, we will need to observe each of these distinct instances multiple times. This is clearly unrealistic in most practical learning domains.

A simple approach to reduce the sample complexity and the problem of estimating $P(\boldsymbol{x}|y)$ is to assume that each feature is independent of the values of the other features given y. This independence assumption is encoded by the equation:

$$P(\boldsymbol{x}|y_i) = \prod_{j=1}^{n} P(x_j|y_i) \tag{1.4}$$

Probabilistic classifiers that use this assumption are called Naive Bayes classifiers [14]. Although the assumption of independence between features rarely holds in real-world applications, they can often outperform more sophisticated classifiers on many data sets.

1.2.2 Linear Classifiers

Suppose we have a training set with real-valued inputs, i.e., $\boldsymbol{x} \in \mathcal{R}^n$, and there are two possible classes, $y \in \{-1, +1\}$. The way binary linear classifiers work is simple: they compute a linear combination of inputs, and determine whether or not the value is larger than some threshold. Therefore, the prediction y can be computed as follows:

$$\begin{aligned} \boldsymbol{w} \cdot \boldsymbol{x} &> \theta, \quad \text{if } y = +1 \\ &< \theta, \quad \text{if } y = -1 \end{aligned} \tag{1.5}$$

Hence, the problem of building a linear classifier is the problem of learning the optimal weight vector $\boldsymbol{w}$ from training data for this classification rule. Geometrically, a linear classifier corresponds to a hyperplane such that the positive instances lie on one side, and negative instances lie on the other side. The weight $\boldsymbol{w}$ is the normal to this hyperplane.

The classifier in equation 1.5 may readily be converted into the corresponding one in which the threshold θ is taken to be zero. It can be proved that for any hyperplane $\boldsymbol{w} \cdot \boldsymbol{x} = \theta$ in $\mathcal{R}^n$, there exists a unique hyperplane in $\boldsymbol{w} \cdot \tilde{\boldsymbol{x}} = 0$ in $\mathcal{R}^{n+1}$ that passes through the origin. Instead of searching for both an n-dimensional weight vector along with a threshold θ, we can search for an $(n+1)$-dimensional weight vector along with an anticipated threshold of zero. Under this assumption, the training error rate for a linear classifier with weight vector $\boldsymbol{w}$ is given by:

$$\frac{1}{n} \sum_{i=1}^{N} s(\boldsymbol{w} \cdot x_i, y_i) \tag{1.6}$$

where s is the step function:

$$s(z) = \begin{cases} 1 & \text{if } z \leq 0 \\ 0 & \text{if } z > 0 \end{cases}$$

In the early statistical literature, the weights were obtained by using linear discriminant analysis (LDA), which makes the assumption that each class has a Gaussian distribution [12]. Similar to linear discriminant analysis, an approach widely used in statistics (usually for regression rather than classification) is the least square fit algorithm. Without any assumption on the underlying distribution, a linear separator can be obtained by using the perceptron scheme that minimizes the training error [15]. Another commonly used approach in statistics for obtaining a linear classifier is logistic regression [16].

1.2.3 Support Vector Machines

SVMs are a popular and well studied technique for classification and regression tasks [17]. In a binary classification problem, SVM aims to find an optimal separating hyperplane which maximizes the margin between different classes of the training data. To do this, SVM first transforms input data into a higher dimensional space (feature space) by means of a kernel function and then constructs a linear optimal hyperplane between the two classes in the transformed space. Those data vectors nearest to the constructed line in the transformed space are called the support vectors (SVs). SVM is an approximate implementation of the method of "structural risk minimization" aiming to attain low probability of generalization error.

In brief, the theory of SVMs is as follows [18]. Consider constructing an SVM based on training data, which consist of N pairs $(x_1, y_1), \cdots, (x_N, y_N)$, for n-dimensional features and associated outcomes $y_i \in \{-1, 1\}$. Each input x_i is first mapped into a higher dimensional feature space $\mathcal{F}$ by $z = \phi(x)$ via a nonlinear mapping $\phi : \mathcal{R}^n \to \mathcal{F}$. Define a hyperplane in the feature space by:

$$w \cdot z + b = 0$$

subject to the constraints:

$$y_i(w \cdot z_i + b) \geq 1 \quad i = 1 \cdots N \tag{1.7}$$

By maximizing the margin of separation between the classes ($\frac{2}{\|w\|}$), an SVM constructs a unique optimal separating hyper plane as the one that minimizes $\frac{w \cdot w}{2}$ under the constraints 1.7. Searching the optimal hyper plane in 1.7 is a quadratic programming (QP) problem that can be solved by constructing a Lagrangian and transforming into the following dual problem:

$$\text{maximize} \quad W(\alpha) = \sum_{i=1}^{N} \alpha_i - \frac{1}{2} \sum_{i=1}^{N} \sum_{j=1}^{N} \alpha_i \alpha_j y_i y_j z_i \cdot z_j$$

$$\text{subject to} \quad \sum_{i=1}^{N} \alpha_i y_i \text{ and } 0 \leq \alpha_i \leq C \; \forall i \tag{1.8}$$

where $\alpha = (\alpha_1, \cdots, \alpha_N)$ is the nonnegative Lagrangian multiplier. The data points x_i corresponding to $\alpha_i > 0$ lie along the margins of the decision boundary and are SVs. $\mathcal{C}$ is a constant parameter, called regularization parameter, which determines the trade-off between the maximum margin and minimum classification error.

The term $z_i \cdot z_j$ in 1.8 can be computed by using a kernel function $K(\cdot, \cdot)$ without having to obtain $\phi(x_i)$ and $\phi(x_j)$ such that

$$z_i \cdot z_j = \phi(x_i) \cdot (x_j) = K(x_i, x_j)$$

Having determined the optimum Lagrange multipliers, the optimum solution for the weight vector w is given by

$$w = \sum_{i=1}^{N} \alpha_i y_i z_i \qquad (1.9)$$

For any test vector $x_i \in \mathcal{R}^n$, the output is then given by

$$y = \text{sign}\Big(\sum_{i \in \text{SVs}} \alpha_i y_i K(x_i, x) + b \Big) \qquad (1.10)$$

To construct SVMs, users must select a kernel function $K(\cdot, \cdot)$. However, there is no way to know *a priori* which kernel is best for a specific pattern recognition problem. The only way to choose the best kernel is through trials. Some commonly used kernel functions include:

Linear function $K(x_i, x_j) = x_i \cdot x_j$

Polynomial function $K(x_i, x_j) = (x_i \cdot x_j + b)^d$

Radial Basis function $K(x_i, x_j) = \exp -\Big(\dfrac{\|(x_i - x_j)\|^2}{2\sigma^2} \Big)$

1.2.4 Random Forests

Tree-based learning algorithms are one of the most widely used learning methods. Random Forest [19] is one such tree-based algorithm which is built using several decision trees. The process of combining classification trees, and classifiers in general, is called an ensemble method. The underlying idea is that combining the results of different classifiers will improve classification and indeed random forests are currently a popular way of implementing classification. In random forests, a classification is obtained for the feature vector x from each tree, which is considered as a vote for the class. The most voted class is selected by the forest for the given vector.

Consider a set $\mathcal{T} = \{(\boldsymbol{x}_i, y_i)\}_{i=1}^{N}$ of target and features; s samples of size N, namely $T_1, T_2, \cdots, T_s$, are selected from $\mathcal{T}$. This sample selection is performed by random sampling with replacement, i.e., for creating each dataset T_i $(i = 1, \cdots, s)$, N number of vectors are selected at random. As random sampling is done with replacement, any instance $(\boldsymbol{x}_i, y_i)$ can be selected several times for different T_i and some instances can be never selected for any T_i.

This is called bagging, from *b*ootstrap *agg*regating [20, 21]. For each T_i, a tree S_i is formed. A new input vector $\boldsymbol{x}_i$ is classified by passing it through s trees. Each tree votes for a particular class for the new vector $\boldsymbol{x}_i$, and the majority vote decides its final class.

Generally, random forest classifiers use two thirds of the input dataset as training set and the rest of the dataset is treated as test data. This one-third data is called out-of-bag data. Estimation of misclassification error is calculated on this test database details can be found in [19, 20]

1.2.5 Neural Networks

Artificial neural networks (ANNs) are inspired by the parallel architecture of the human brain and based on the operation of biological neural networks. They contain a series of mathematical equations that are used to simulate biological processes such as learning and memory [22].

Although they are biologically inspired, ANNs can be analyzed from a purely statistical viewpoint [10, 23]. In this way, ANNs can be regarded as statistical algorithms capable of modeling complex, nonlinear relationships among variables. More specifically, given a sample $\mathcal{T} = \{(\boldsymbol{x}_i, y_i)\}_{i=1}^{N}$ generated by an unknown function $f(\boldsymbol{x})$ (plus an additive stochastic component), i.e.,

$$y_i = f(\boldsymbol{x}_i) + \epsilon_i \tag{1.11}$$

the role of the network is to construct an estimator $g(\boldsymbol{x}, \boldsymbol{w})$ of $f(\boldsymbol{x})$, where $\boldsymbol{w} = (w_1, \cdots, w_\tau)$ is a set of free parameters (known as "connection weights"). From this perspective, an ANN is simply a function, $g(\boldsymbol{x}, \boldsymbol{w})$, that defines an approximation from input to output.

The three essential features of an ANN are 1) the basic processing elements referred to as neurons or nodes; 2) the network architecture describing the connections between nodes; and 3) the training algorithm used to find values of the network's parameters for performing a particular task. Our discussion is restricted to

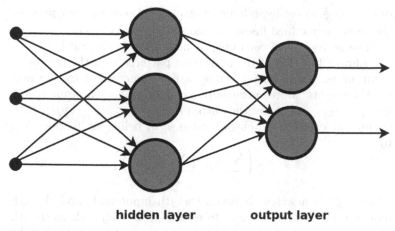

hidden layer   **output layer**

Figure 1.2 Example of a multi-layer neural network architecture.

supervised neural networks, that is, cases where there is a known target or outcome variable to train the models [23].

Specifically, the nodes of the network are organized in layers (see Figure 1.2). The layers between the input and the output layers are called "hidden". The number of input units is determined by the application. The lines between the nodes indicate the flow of information from one node to the next. As shown in Figure 1.2, for a typical feedforward network, the information flows only from the input to the output, meaning that there are no loops in the network, that is, there are no paths within the network by which a unit's output can influence its input [24]. As we will see later in chapter 2, if the network contains loops, it is a recurrent or feedback network rather than a feedforward network. In this chapter we make references only to the feedforward network model.

The nodes of input layer are passive, meaning they do not modify the data. They receive a single value on their input, and duplicate the value to their multiple outputs. For the other layers, the nodes are semi-linear units, meaning that they compute a weighted sum of their input signals and then apply to the result a nonlinear function, called the *activation function*, to produce the unit's output or activation. Different activation functions ϕ are used, but they are typically sigmoidal functions such as the logistic function

$\phi(x) = \frac{1}{(1+e^{-x})}$, or hyperbolic tangent functions; another popular choice is the rectified linear function $f(x) = \max(0, x)$.

The activation of each output node of a feedforward ANN is a nonlinear function of the activation patterns over the network's input units. These output values are parameterized by the network's weights. More specifically, given an unknown input vector $x = (x_1, x_2, \cdots, x_n)$ and the output set $y = \{y_1, y_2, \cdots, y_M\}$, each output node yields the output value $\hat{y}_i$ of belonging to this class by:

$$\hat{y}_i = \phi\left\{ \sum_k w_{ik}^{om} \left(\sum_j w_{kj}^{mi} x_j \right) \right\} \quad (1.12)$$

where w_{kj}^{mi} is a weight between the jth input node and the kth hidden node, w_{ik}^{om} is a weight from the kth hidden node to the ith class output, and ϕ is the activation function. The node having the maximum value is selected as the corresponding class.

ANNs typically learn by a stochastic gradient method. The weights in the network are adjusted in a direction aimed at improving the overall performance of the network as measured by an objective function to be either minimized or maximized. In the most common supervised learning case, the objective function is the expected error, or loss, over a set of labeled training. In all the cases, it is necessary to estimate how a change in each connection weight would influence the overall performance of the network, in other words, to estimate the partial derivative of an objective function with respect to each weight, given the current value of all the network's weights. The backpropagation algorithm is the most popular way to do this [7]. It consists of two different phases, i.e. the forward phase and the backward phase. In the forward phase, the input signals are computed and passed through the neural network layer by layer. After the neurons in the output layer generate the output signals, the error signals will be generated by comparing the output response with the desired response. Then, in the backward phase, the error is propagated back to each neuron, and the relative weights are adjusted accordingly in order to reduce the error. More information on backpropagation can be found in [7,25].

CHAPTER 2

Introduction to Deep Learning

The term *Deep Learning* refers to a particular class of neural networks where many layers, from five or seven layers up to several hundreds, are stacked on top of each other [26]. Unlike their shallow counterparts, which are introduced in Chapter 1, deep neural networks can directly process raw input data, including images, text and sound. They directly uncover low and high-level features from the training data, an approach which is generally denoted as *representation learning* in the relevant literature. Consequently, the feature extraction and selection process is significantly simplified, or better automated. Most importantly, neuron-crafted features have often proven to surpass the discriminative power of conventional feature extraction methods. Hand-crafted features are often based on heuristics or simplifications of the objects or patterns that we wish to detect, and are limited by our ability to capture the full spectrum of the statistical variability that such patterns exhibit in practice. This is particular true for visual tasks, which humans often perform intuitively and learn from examples and experience, rather than formally. Deep learning enables us precisely that: to teach machines how to see by showing examples.

The foundation of deep learning in artificial vision is the *convolutional neural network*, which was first introduced in the seminal paper by LeCun in 1998 [27]. However, at the time training algorithms, as well as computational resources, allowed for a limited number of intermediate layers. The availability of faster CPUs and general purpose Graphical Processing Units (GPUs), and improvements in training algorithms, have enabled researchers to train increasingly larger models on increasingly larger datasets, laying the basis for the current success of deep learning [25]. In this chapter we will present the main principles behind the design and training of a modern deep neural network, starting with an overview of the main architectures of interest for the computer vision community in general, and for the medical domain in particular. Medical use cases and applications will be covered in more detail in Chapter 3.

2.1 DEEP LEARNING NETWORK ARCHITECTURES

Deep learning network architectures are not created equal. Over time, it became apparent that certain structures were particularly apt at modelling specific types of input: Convolutional Neural Networks (CNNs), for instance, are specifically designed for images, whereas Recurrent Neural Networks (RNNs) can model sequences. Such architectures exploit inductive biases, that is general assumptions about the properties of the observed data, allowing generalization to new unseen examples.

A schematic representation of the most common architectures in medical image analysis is presented in Figure 2.1. According to a recent survey by Litjens and colleagues [28], CNN is the most common architecture in medical image analysis. It can be used directly for image classification, or it can form the backbone of more sophisticated architectures for object detection, classification, visual captioning and so forth. In this chapter, we will review CNNs and briefly touch upon RNNs. Probabilistic architectures, such as Restricted Boltzmann machines, are less used in practice and will be skipped in this brief introduction; the interested reader is referred to excellent textbooks such as the one by Ian Goodfellow, Yoshua Bengio and Aaron Courville [25].

2.1.1 Feedforward Neural Networks

Feedforward neural networks, introduced in Section 1.2.5, are the simplest form of neural network. They are comprised of two or more feedforward layers; the most common architectural choice is the Fully Connected (FC) layer, where all neurons have full connections to all the activations in the previous layer.

Let us recall that that the output of each layer k is given by:

$$\hat{y}_k = \phi\left(\mathbf{W}_k^{\mathbf{T}}\mathbf{y}_{\mathbf{k-1}} + b_k\right) \tag{2.1}$$

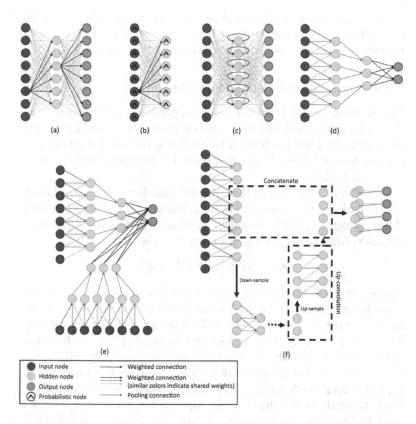

Figure 2.1 Node graphs of one-dimensional representations of architectures commonly used in medical imaging. (a) Auto-encoder, (b) restricted Boltzmann machine, (c) recurrent neural network, (d) convolutional neural network, (e) multi-stream convolutional neural network, (f) U-net (with a single downsampling stage). Modified from Litjens, Geert, et al. "A survey on deep learning in medical image analysis." *Medical Image Analysis* 42 (2017): 60-88. [28]

where W_k and b are the weights and bias of the k-th layer, y_k is the output of the the k-th layer, and ϕ is the non linear activation function.

FC layers are generally employed as last layers to learn classification functions, but given their large number of parameters their importance has gradually reduced in modern architectures.

2.1.2 Convolutional Neural Networks

Convolutional neural networks are specialized architectures designed to learn good feature representations for multidimensional array signals. They are formed by a sequence of convolutional and pooling layers, followed by one or more FC layers to learn the classification boundary.

Its core building block, the convolutional layer, consists of a set of learnable convolutional filters (also known as *kernels*), each with shape (height $\times$ width $\times$ depth). The output feature $\mathbf{X}_k^l$ is thus obtained from the input feature map $\mathbf{X}_{k-1}$ as follows:

$$\mathbf{X_k} = \sigma(\mathbf{W_k^l} * \mathbf{X_{k-1}^{l-1}} + b_k^l) \tag{2.2}$$

where k denotes the feature index, l denotes the layer and $*$ is the convolution operator. An additional *stride* parameter controls the amount of pixels or unit by which the filter moves while convolving. The default value is $(1,1)$; higher strides (e.g. $(2,2)$) can be used, with the effect that the feature map will be downsampled.

Usually, the height and width dimensions are fixed and small, typical values ranging from $(1,1)$ to $(7,7)$; the depth dimension extends through the full depth of the input volume. Since the seminal work by Simonyan, deeper networks are usually preferred [29]. During training, the network learns the filters that generate higher response to specific classes of interest. A two-dimensional activation map is created for each filter and a stack of these maps becomes the output of each layer.

Convolutional networks are based on three main assumptions: the output of each filter depends only on a local region of the input (*locality*), all local regions share the same parameter values (*stationarity*), and each layer takes as input the output of previous layers (*compositionality*).

The first two properties imply that the network does not need to learn separate detectors or features for objects occurring at different positions within an image. It also drastically reduces the number of parameters to be learned, and it has the useful property that the number of parameters does not depend on the size of the input image.

As said, each neuron is connected to a small region in the previous layer. This local region is called the *receptive field* of the neuron; it is equal to the filter size at the first layer, and depends on the filter sizes and network depth at following layers [28]. A receptive field that is too small may hinder the detection of lesions as some context is usually beneficial for detection.

Deep neural networks exploit the property that many natural signals are compositional hierarchies, in which higher–level features are obtained by composing lower–level ones. In images, local combinations of edges form motifs, motifs assemble into parts, and parts form objects [26].

Low-level layers in the hierarchy tend to learn simple, general purpose features, such as edges and colors, whereas subsequent layers learn complex, task and domain-dependent features [30]. Convolutional layers impose very few a priori properties on learned features: in fact, only equivariance with respect to translations is assured.

Understanding how features in an image are modeled by a CNN is a hot topic of research, and one of the most common approaches is to provide visual "explanations". These visualization techniques are helpful to optimize CNN training and ensure that the CNN is "paying attention" to the correct regions of an image in analysis. Popular methods for visualization include activation heatmaps, perturbation-based methods, backpropagation-based methods and visualization of feature spaces [31, 32]. As an example, let us consider backpropagation-based methods: they work by measuring gradients of the output with respect to the input in order to construct heatmaps that identify the importance of each pixel with respect to the final output. Examples of back-propagation-based methods include Layer-wise Relevance Propagation (LRP), guided back-propagation, and gradient-weighted Class Activation Map (GradCAM). Examples can be seen in Figures 2.2 and 3.1.

A common practice in CNN architecture design is to periodically intersperse convolutional and pooling layers. By reducing the spatial dimensions of the input, pooling decreases the computational power and parameters required to train the network. As a consequence, the risk of overfitting is also reduced. A pooling layer downsamples each input feature independently; common pooling strategies are max-pooling and average-pooling, where each patch

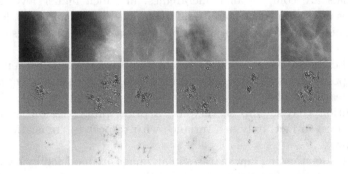

Figure 2.2 Visualization techniques are the most common means to understand how a convolutional neural network "looks" at an image. This example refers to a VGG-16 network trained to detect microcalcification clusters in mammography patches (top row). Guided back-propagation (middle row) and layer-wise relevance propagation (bottom row) are used to identify which pixels are most relevant to the classification task. Note how the microcalcifications are highlighted in the relevance maps, regardless of the background.

of neighboring cells is assigned the maximum or average value in the patch itself.

Pooling also introduces a certain degree of invariance to small shifts and distortions, since the output activations are less sensitive to the relative positions of the input features that form a certain motif. It also enlarges the receptive field of subsequent convolutional layers. The downside of pooling layers is that the network loses the ability to accurately model spatial relationship [33]. They also reduce spatial resolution and hence may impact the ability to detect small objects [34].

Since the early 2000's, the performance of CNN-based vision systems has caused most major technology companies, including Google, Facebook, Microsoft, IBM, Yahoo!, Twitter and Adobe, as well as a quickly growing number of start-ups, to initiate research and development projects and to deploy CNN-based image understanding products and services. A substantial amount of research has been devoted to the identification of CNN architectures that obtain high performance, usually based on benchmarks such as the ImageNet large scale recognition challenge [35, 36].

Engineering a new architecture is time consuming and computationally intensive. When tackling a new task, it is common practice to start with a known architecture and then modify it, rather than design a new one from scratch for each novel task. This practice is supported by the intuition, backed by solid experimental evidence at least in the natural image domain, that models that perform better on ImageNet also perform better on other datasets [37]. It should be noticed that state-of-the-art architectures in computer vision are usually very deep, with hundreds of layers. In medical imaging, where training data is often scarce, shallower architectures such as VGG [29] are still popular choices.

At the time of writing, two particular classes of architectures are worth citing: Residual Networks [38] and Inception Networks [39, 40]. Early CNN architectures were strictly sequential: all inputs are fed through the same filters at each layer, and each layer feeds directly into the next one. During backpropagation, the gradients are calculated by moving layer by layer from the final layer to the initial one; by the chain rule, the derivatives of each layer are multiplied down the network, causing the gradients to become smaller and smaller at each step (the so called *vanishing gradient* issue). For many years, this effectively prevented training of very deep neural networks in a stable way. Several engineering "tricks" have been proposed to alleviate this issue, such as the use of the

Rectified Linear Unit (*ReLU*), which unlike the sigmoid function does not "squash" the derivatives as the output saturates.

Residual networks [38] were also designed in response to the vanishing gradient problem, by feeding each layer not only into the next one, but also in subsequent layers; the standard choice is to skip two layers at a time. During training, the network can effectively modulate the depth of the network, by exploiting skip connections: for each training data point, different parts of networks will be trained at different rates based on how the error flows backwards in the network. Other architectural variants that exploit connections between preceding layers have been proposed, such as highway networks, or the most recent DenseNet addition in which each layer is connected to all preceding layers [41]. Since each layer sees all the feature maps from all preceding layers, the resulting network can be thinner and more compact, hence requiring fewer parameters.

On the other hand, *Inception* modules, first introduced in GoogleNet [39] and Inception ResNet [40], include partitioned structures, based on modules that can perform several operations (i.e. pooling or convolution) in *parallel*. The network is then able to "choose" which operation or kernel size better fits the current data.

2.1.3 Recurrent Neural Networks

Recurrent neural networks (RNNs) are a special type of ANNs which contain loops, thus allowing information to persist over time [25]. This is pivotal to modelling sequences, such as in speech recognition and language modeling.

RNNs process an input sequence one element at a time, maintaining in their hidden units a "state vector" that stores implicit information about the history of all past elements in the sequence. When we consider the outputs of the hidden units at different discrete time steps as if they were the outputs of different neurons in a deep multilayer network, it becomes clear how we can apply backpropagation over time to train RNNs. RNNs are very powerful dynamic systems, but training is difficult because the backpropagated gradients either grow or shrink at each time step, so over many time steps they typically explode or vanish [26].

Long Short-Term Memory (LSTM) networks are one of the most successful RNNs architectures [42]. The core intuition is that each LSTM unit has a cell state, a sort of "memory" which can

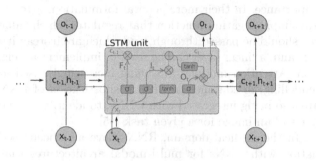

Figure 2.3 Architecture of the Long Short-Term Memory (LSTM) unit. A LSTM network is formed by a sequence of one or more LSTM unit. Image courtesy of François Deloche.

be transferred down the chain to carry relevant information. The LSTM architecture introduces gates that modulate information passed through the network, depending on the value of the current input, maintaining only those elements that are useful, and forgetting irrelevant information. As a result, it becomes easier to model long-term dependencies.

As illustrated in Figure 2.3, each LSTM unit receives as time t the input value X_t and the previous cell state h_{t-1}; it outputs the next cell state h_t and the output value at the current time step o_t.

The *forget* gate F_l allows, as the name implics, to discard the previous cell state h_{t-1} when and to the extent it is no longer useful. Usually a sigmoid activation function is used, so the output of each gate is between 0 and 1. The *input* gate I_t takes as input h_{t-1} and X_t and decides whether input information is relevant to the task at end. The *output* gate O_t produces the final value of the hidden state h_t, regulating the competing influence of memory and current input. An important variant of LSTM is the Convolutional LSTM or ConvLSTM, which replaces matrix multiplications at each gate with convolution operation: thus the input is no longer a scalar, but a three-dimensional feature map which captures underlying spatial features. This variant has been successfully applied to modelling spatio-temporal information in the medical domain, such as predicting tumor growth from sequential CT scans [43].

In recent years, *attention* modules are also gaining widespread importance. In their more general formulation, attention modules are simply a gating function that regulates which values in an array should be passed through, and which are instead irrelevant. To this aim, a linear layer can be used to implement a weighting function. Attention modules are being increasingly used for sequence modelling, in conjunction with or substitution of RNNs [44], and are also being integrated with CNNs, to identify the most relevant parts of an image for a given task [45].

In the medical domain, RNNs have also been used in combination with CNNs for multi-modal architectures that can learn from text and images, as will be introduced in Section 2.1.6. An example of such applications is biomedical image captioning, in which a descriptive caption is produced directly from an image, without resorting to intermediate steps [46]. Radiology departments generate large quantities of digital content in the form of free-text clinical narratives, on which natural language processing techniques, including but not limited to deep neural networks, can be applied [47].

2.1.4 Object Detection Network

The standard CNN is able to determine whether the input image contains a specific pattern (e.g., a lesion or anatomical structure). Object detection networks are able to locate multiple targets within an image, not only by assigning a label but also by predicting the location of a bounding box around the object of interest. The most recent architectures are also able to provide a segmentation of each object of interest. They are thus a very interesting architecture for many diagnostic tasks that involve not only classification but also localization of disease patterns [48–50].

Since it is not possible to determine a priori the number of objects to be detected, this problem cannot be solved by using a standard fully convolutional network. A brute force approach would be to take different regions of interest from the image and use a CNN to classify the presence of the object within that region. The issue with this approach is that objects of interest may have different spatial positions within the image and different aspect ratios, resulting in an exponential number of possible regions.

To circumvent this problem, several object detectors such as Faster R-CNN, RetinaNet, and YOLO have been developed to quickly identify potential areas of interest. These architectures fall within two groups: two-stage proposal-driven detectors, and one-pass detectors.

As popularized in the R-CNN framework, two–stage architectures first generate a sparse set of candidate object locations, and the second stage classifies each candidate location as one of the foreground classes or as background using a convolutional neural network. The Faster RCNN is one of the highest performing architecture in this category [51]. It is composed of two modules: a fully convolutional object proposal network known as the Region Proposal Network (RPN), and a detector. The RPN is applied over a regular, dense sampling of object locations, scales, and aspect ratios, to generate a list of initial object candidates, which are then classified by the detector in one of the available classes. The two modules have shared convolutional layers, which are usually initialized with pre-trained weights. Each "head" of the network has two outputs: a classification score (binary "objectness" score for the RPN, and multiclass classification for the detector) and a regression output, which provides the coordinates of the bounding box, adapted to the specific content. A multi-objective loss is optimized during training:

$$L(\{p_i\}, \{b_i\}) = \frac{1}{N_r} \sum_i L_{cls}(p_i, p_i') + \lambda \frac{1}{N_c} \sum_i L_{reg}(b_i, b_i') \quad (2.3)$$

where L_{reg} is a regression loss that accounts for the difference between the predicted bounding box b_i' and the ground truth bounding box b_i, and the classification loss L_{cls}, usually categorical cross entropy, depends on the difference between the predicted p_i' and true probabilities p_i of the bounding box containing a lesion. The two terms are normalized by N_c (equals to the mini-batch size) and N_r (which depends on the number of anchors), and weighted by a balancing parameter λ. Example of object detection networks applied to mammography are provided in Chapter 3.

One–stage detectors like YOLO [52] and RetinaNet [53] are applied directly over the regular, dense grid, and simultaneously perform classification and predict regression parameters. This results in a highly imbalanced classification problem, as the background is by far more abundant than objects in general, and than any specific class in particular. To cope with the absence of the RPN,

RetinaNet solves this problem by introducing a loss function which is particularly robust to class imbalance.

Many single-stage detectors include a Feature Pyramid Network (FPN) as the backbone network: in brief, FPN augments a standard CNN with lateral connections to extract a multi-scale feature pyramid from a single resolution input image. This allows the system to cope with objects of different scales and dimensions. One–stage detectors are faster than two–stage detectors, and are usually considered less accurate, although more recent architectures achieve competitive results [53].

Predicting the location of a lesion or abnormality is a useful feature for many medical imaging applications. This however does not require us to frame the problem within the object detection framework. For classification networks that take as input an entire image and output a possible diagnostic label (e.g. positive or negative), an alternative strategy is to employ visualization or attribution techniques to explain the decisions made by the classification network [54–57].

2.1.5 Segmentation Network

The segmentation of organs, lesions or other substructures is an important task in medical image analysis, as will be discussed in Chapter 3. The task of segmentation is typically defined as identifying the set of voxels[1] which make up either the contour or the interior of the object(s) of interest. Segmentation is one of the most common subjects of papers applying deep learning to medical imaging [28], and as such a large variety of CNN and RNN-based architectures have been proposed here.

In the most naive implementation, CNNs can simply be used to classify each pixel in the image individually, by presenting it with patches extracted around the particular pixel. More interestingly, it has been shown that fully connected layers can be rewritten as convolutions: the resulting fully convolutional network (FCNN) can be trained on individual patches or image subsections, and then efficiently applied at test time on images of arbitrary size, producing as output a likelihood map of each region belonging to the structure of interest. However, because of pooling layers, the output may have a far lower resolution than the input.

---

[1]The term voxel denotes a pixel volumetric imaging, where each image element is three-dimensional.

A very popular architecture for segmentation problems is the U-Net and its variants [58, 59]: an example is shown Figure 2.4. This architecture is a variant of the encoder-decoder architecture, where the network takes as input the original image or volume, and learns to reconstruct the segmentation as output. A combination of downsampling and upsampling layers are used to learn opposing contracting and expanding convolutional layers, thus allowing the output to retain the full resolution. The network is trained by minimizing the cross-entropy function between the pixel-wise segmentation labels and the network output.

One challenge with voxel classification approaches is that they sometimes lead to spurious responses, and do not fully exploit the correlation between neighboring pixels. This motivates the application of RNNs which model neighboring pixels as elements in a sequence. Alternatively, many groups have tried to combine FCNNs with graphical models like Conditional Random Fields, which are applied on top of the likelihood map produced by CNNs or FCNNs and act as label regularizers [28, 60].

2.1.6 Multi-stream and Multi-modal Architectures

The default CNN architecture can easily accommodate multiple sources of information or representations of the input, in the form of channels presented to the input layer. Each channel can be processed by the same or by separate convolutional layers for feature extraction. Depending on the task and on the similarity of the inputs, channels can be merged at any point in the network, finding the optimal balance between feature specialization, on one hand, and reducing the number of parameters, on the other hand.

In computer vision multi-stream architectures serve different purposes. For instance, they have been extensively used in video analysis to include both spatial and temporal features [62]. In medical imaging, video analysis is less common (with notable exceptions such as endoscopy video), but mixing spatial and temporal features can find applications in the modeling of temporal sequences [43,63].

In the medical domain, multi-stream architectures have found important applications such as multi-scale image analysis and analysis of three-dimensional (volumetric) datasets. They stem from the necessity to bridge the limitation of current neural networks frameworks and hardware, particularly GPU memory. At the moment, the amount of memory available for computation is usually limited compared to the image size of many imaging modalities, es-

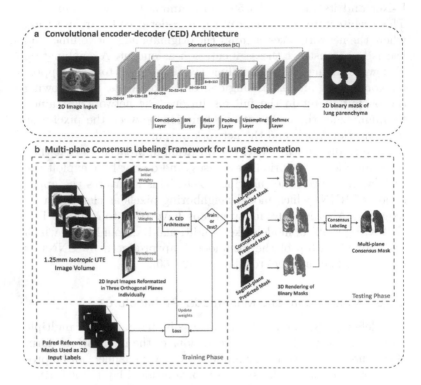

Figure 2.4   Example of segmentation network based on the encoder/decoder principle. Note how each pooling layer is compensated by a corresponding upsampling layer to maintain the final resolution. To cope with the three-dimensionality of the input data, three views are generated from the coronal, axial and sagittal planes, which divide the patient body across orthogonal axes. The resulting maps are then combined to generate a three-dimensional segmentation map. Modified from Zha, Wei, et al. "Deep convolutional neural networks with multiplane consensus labeling for lung function quantification using UTE proton MRI." *Journal of Magnetic Resonance Imaging* (2019). [61]

pecially histopathology and volumetric images, and this limitation is unlikely to be completely solved in the near future. Downsampling can reduce the size of the feature maps, but may lead to the loss of useful diagnostic features. Multi-stream architectures may solve this conundrum, extracting each input channel at different resolutions to provide both local and global context [64, 65].

The approach denoted as 2.5D convolution was born out of the necessity to adapt convolutional neural networks developed or pretrained on 2D (natural) images to 3D volumes. As an alternative to use heavy 3D convolutional filters, which are nonetheless becoming more widespread in recent years, the volume of interest can be represented by slices at different planes, which are then fed as different streams to a network [66].

Finally, multi-stream architectures are not limited to one single input modality, but can for example mix images from different modalities [67], multiple views [68], or even text and images [69].

2.1.7 Generative Adversarial Networks

Generative models refer to a class of methods to estimate the data distribution $p(X)$, usually by approximating it with a function $\hat{p}_\theta(X)$ parameterized by some parameters θ. Generative models can then be used to draw new, previously unseen samples from this distribution. Many generative models have been proposed, but the most popular are Generative Adversarial Networks (GANs), first presented in 2014 by Goodfellow and colleagues [70], which have gained high popularity as the images they generate are usually higher quality and more realistic. Training GANs is not an easy feat as the process is highly unstable and may collapse to degenerate solutions. However, much progress has been made to stabilize their training and GANs are now able to achieve impressive results. So far, they have found applications in the medical domain in data augmentation, domain adaptation, image synthesis from multiple modalities, segmentation and anomaly detection, although it must be noticed that such applications are mostly at a research stage [71, 72].

GANs achieve this goal by combining two neural networks, the generator G and the discriminator D, which compete against each other during training (thus the name "adversarial"). The potential of this framework is huge, because it can in principle learn to mimic any input distribution (images, text, and so forth) and use it to generate novel samples. More precisely, the generator decodes a random vector into a synthetic image; this generated image is fed into the discriminator alongside a stream of images taken from the actual, ground-truth dataset, and the discriminator tries to classify whether the generated image is real or fake.

GANs are based on a competitive minimax game rather than on the optimization of a single loss function: the objective is a value function that one agent seeks to maximize, and the other seeks to minimize. The game terminates at a saddle point that is a minimum with respect to one player's strategy and a maximum with respect to the other player's strategy or, in simple terms, when the generator is able to fool the discriminator. At inference time, only the generator is used.

Of particular interest for the medical domain is the class of conditional GANs, which extend the original formulation by embedding an additional input along with the noise to the generator. This additional input can be for instance a class label (usually a one-hot encoded vector). They allow for much greater control over the final output from the generator by allowing the model to differentiate between different classes, or even to model image-to-image translation, such as in CycleGAN [71, 73].

Uses of GANs in the medical domain are plentiful. The ability to synthetize novel samples is useful in data augmentation and domain adaptation, which will be reviewed in Chapter 2.2. Image-to-image GANs have also been successfully applied to segmentation tasks.

An example of medical image synthesis through GANs is illustrated in Figure 2.5. The proposed network is trained to synthetize magnetic resonance images. An image-to-image translation conditional GAN (`pix2pix`) is first used to segment normal brain anatomy from anatomical MR images (MRI-to-brain segmentation): the GAN is trained to generate segmentation masks, conditioned on a given MR image, and the discriminator tries to distinguish ground truth from synthesized masks. The synthetic image generation is trained on the inverse task (label-to-MRI segmentation): the input is a tumor segmentation mask, and the output is the corresponding MR scan. Finally, a third network is trained to generate the tumor mask from MR scans (image-to-tumor segmentation). The proposed network can be used to generate novel images: for example, a tumor mask can be manipulated in several ways, e.g. by enlarging its size; the tumor mask is then merged with a normal anatomy, and input to the label-to-MRI segmentation to produce synthetic scans, as shown in Figure 2.5.

2.2 TRAINING NEURAL NETWORKS FOR MEDICAL IMAGES

Like any other discriminative model, a neural network can be trained in a supervised, unsupervised or semi-supervised fashion, as introduced in Chapter 1. A practical guide to training neural networks is beyond the scope of this book, and we refer the reader to the many resources available in the form of textbooks, courses and online material [25, 75–78].

We briefly touch here on fundamental aspects such as hyper-parameter optimization and data augmentation, and provide an overview of topics which are at the forefront of deep learning research, such as transfer learning and domain adaptation.

One of the fundamental issues in applying deep learning to medical imaging is solving the limited training size problem. This problem has been tackled from several angles by the AI/ML community. For instance, we will review the possibilities offered by transfer and multi-task learning. An important problem in ML is in fact how to re-use knowledge about one task to learn other tasks more efficiently, which reduces the amount of labelled data required to train a deep network, and has been pivotal in the diffusion of convolutional neural networks. We will close this chapter with a brief overview of unsupervised and semi-supervised learning.

2.2.1 Hyper-parameter Search

The process of training a deep neural network requires choosing its architecture and hyper-parameters. While many de-facto standard architectures have emerged in computer vision, as previously discussed in Chapter 2.1.2, finding the best architecture for a given task still requires extensive experimentation and expertise, as well as vast computational resources.

Furthermore, training a deep neural network through stochastic gradient descent requires optimizing several hyper-parameters, such as the learning rate and mini-batch size; this is a painstaking and non trivial iterative process, often severely constrained by time and computational resources. The correct choice of hyper-parameters on a proper validation set is paramount to achieve optimal performance, often trumping the benefits of more complex

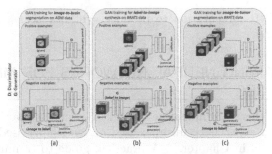

(a) image-to-image conditionalGANs

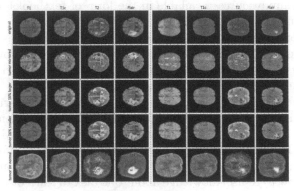

(b) Synthetic MRI scans

Figure 2.5 Example of GAN architecture and generated synthetic brain MR scans. (a) Illustration of training GAN for MRI-to-brain segmentation; label-to-MRI synthesis; and MRI-to-tumor segmentation. (b) The first row depicts the original ("real") images on which the synthetic tumors were based. Generated images without adjustment of the segmentation label are shown in the second row. Examples of generated images with various adjustments to the tumor segmentation label are shown in the third through fifth rows. The last row depicts examples of synthetic images where a tumor label is placed on a tumor-free brain label from the ADNI data set. Images reproduced from Shin, Hoo-Chang, et al. "Medical image synthesis for data augmentation and anonymization using generative adversarial networks." *International Workshop on Simulation and Synthesis in Medical Imaging.* Springer, 2018. [74]

architectures. This motivates a large body of research on optimization of neural network training, with a specific focus on optimizing the learning rate schedule [25, 79, 80].

Manual intuition-based search is arguably the most commonly used technique to optimize the model and hyper-parameters, because it is easy to implement and exploits researchers' experience to reduce the number of trials, which is useful when training large networks that require extensive computational resources [28]. Nonetheless, in recent years there has been increasing interest in meta-learning or self-supervising strategies that can automate the process of model selection and training, which goes under the name of Automated Machine Learning or AutoML.

Possible AutoML strategies for deep learning include random hyper-parameter search [81], evolutionary strategies for neural network configuration such as the NEAT and HyperNEAT algorithms [82, 83] and Bayesian optimization [84–86]. So far, their use in deep learning, and especially high resolution image analysis, has been restricted to research groups and industries with large computational facilities, but this may change in the future as such strategies become more effective and require less data or training rounds to converge.

The problem of hyper-parameter selection is not new, and applies also to traditional image processing pipelines. Likewise, the most common approach is through manual tuning until accurate results on a representative dataset are reached. Nonetheless, genetic algorithms and evolutionary strategies were successfully applied both in medical imaging [64, 87–89] and bioinformatics [90]. The advantage of such approaches is that they do not require an analytic formulation of the function to be optimized, and hence are applicable to any kind of processing pipeline regardless of the implementation. However, practical implementations require large computational resources and have found limited applications.

2.2.2 Data Augmentation

Deep learning relies heavily on high quality annotated data, which is often limited by the cost and complexity of acquisition. Even when a large dataset is available, it only contains a finite set of samples of a much larger data distribution. Furthermore, the dataset may be skewed towards a specific class (data imbalance) or towards certain populations or acquisition parameters. In a nutshell, it is challenging to construct a well balanced training set, and even more challenging to predict which features the training process will extract from a dataset. Data augmentation refers to a broad set of techniques that expand the original set of samples, usually at training time, to improve the quality of the dataset and enhance the generalization capabilities of the network.

The simplest form of data augmentation consists in generating new images from existing data by applying random transformation to the original dataset. It was first introduced by Krizhevsky on the ImageNet dataset, and is now a standard part of training CNNs [91]. These transformations include random translations, rotations and flips, noise injection, contrast enhancement and so forth. Such methods capitalize on transformations that we know should not affect the class, in order to render convolutional features robust with respect to them. Data augmentation acts as a regularizer, and has been found to be beneficial regardless of the size of the dataset. Furthermore, it is crucial to make the network invariant to factors such as rotation, scale, and intensity variations.

However, in order for data augmentation to be effective, the transformed images need to be consistent with the original distribution. Due to the differences between medical images and natural images, many transformations that are effective in one domain may be useless or even harmful in the other.

In more recent years, the concept of learnable data augmentation strategies is emerging as a powerful tool to push CNNs performance. These strategies include, for example, the automatic optimization of data transformation policies in order to generate progressively harder samples [92, 93]. Generative adversarial networks are another very promising technique for generating artificial work samples, as illustrated in Section 2.1.7. The advantage of GANs is that they can be conditioned to generate specific types of samples, and hence may be used to alleviate known biases in the training data. However, practitioners need to be aware that GANs may hallucinate image features that mimic or mask the presence of lesions [94].

2.2.3 Transfer Learning

An important problem in ML is how to re-use knowledge about one task to learn other tasks more efficiently, which is one of the hallmarks of human intelligence. This issue is certainly not limited to deep learning, and has been long studied in the wider context of machine learning. At the same time, one of the advantages of representation learning is that it lends itself particularly well to transferring or sharing information across tasks.

Let us a recall that in a standard supervised learning setting, the objective is to learn a mapping function f between the feature space $\mathcal{X}$ and a label space $\mathcal{Y}$, where the pair defines a *task* $\mathcal{T} = \{\mathcal{Y}, f\}$. The mapping function is inferred from pairs of labelled training data (x, y). The *domain*, on the other hand, pertains to the distribution of the input space, and depends on factors such as acquisition parameters, patient population and many others (this concept will be reprised in Chapter 4). Given an input feature space, it is formally defined by the marginal distribution of the input data $\mathcal{D} = \{\mathcal{X}, p(X)\}$. Many standard ML techniques assume that the test data is drawn from the same distribution as the training data and when this assumption does not hold, the performance at test time can be significantly degraded.

The problem of transfer learning can be thus defined formally as the transfer of knowledge from a source task $\mathcal{T}_S$ and domain $\mathcal{D}_S$, to a target task $\mathcal{T}_T$ and domain $\mathcal{D}_T$. Several settings can be identified: same task and different domains, same domain but different tasks, or different tasks and different domains. The special case in which the task remains the same, but the domain is different, is usually denoted as *domain adaptation*, and will be discussed in the next section.

In the case of medical images, the task depends on the pathology or organ targeted, as well as the type of analysis, whether it is classification, detection, segmentation, risk analysis and so forth. The domain depends on the targeted population [95], as well as in differences in the medical imaging modality or acquisition parameters [96]; both factors will change the visual appearance of the lesion or organ of interest, resulting in the so-called *domain shift*. For a more in depth discussion of factors that may affect the performance of AI/ML systems, the reader is referred to Chapter 4.2.2.

There is strong evidence that visual tasks share many common traits, and that learning one task can highly benefit from previous ones [96, 97]. In the transfer learning setting, we generally have a source task for which labelled data is abundant, and a target task with limited training data. Transfer learning approaches addressing these scenarios can be grouped by what they transfer: in this chapter, we will focus mostly on feature transfer, i.e. encoding knowledge from the source domain into the feature representation for the target domain. We refer the reader to existing literature for an analysis of other transfer learning methods [96, 98].

In a deep CNN, feature transfer can be accomplished by simply copying the first n layers of the source network to the first n layers of a target network [30]. The remaining layers of the target network are then randomly initialized and trained towards the target task. Indeed, training a state-of-the-art deep CNNs from random weight initialization requires millions of labelled datapoints and is not common practice.

CNNs trained on natural images usually exhibit a curious phenomenon: on the first layer they learn features similar to Gabor filters and color blobs. Such first-layer features appear not to be specific to a particular dataset or task, whereas features in subsequent layers become increasingly specific. One can choose to back-propagate the errors from the new task into the base (copied) features to fine-tune them to the new task, or the transferred feature layers can be left frozen, meaning that they do not change during training on the new task.

The choice of whether or not to fine-tune the first layers of the target network depends on the size of the target dataset, the number of parameters in the first n layers and the similarity between the two tasks. If the target dataset is small and the number of parameters is large, fine-tuning may result in overfitting, so the features are best left frozen. On the other hand, if the target dataset is large or the number of parameters is small, so that overfitting is not a problem, then the base features can be fine-tuned to the new task to improve performance. Finally, when the target dataset is small but similar to the source data that is used to train the network, extracted features with this network generally produce separable data; as a consequence, training a traditional classifier is usually a good strategy.

The question then becomes largely which source of data can be effectively used for transfer learning within the medical domain: is transfer learning from natural (non medical) images effective? Alternatively, which sources of data can be used?

The answer to the first question is, in general, positive. To date, the most common dataset used for transfer learning is the ImageNet dataset [36]. The dataset has more than a million images and thousand categories of labelled everyday objects: such diversity is difficult to obtain in the medical domain. This methodology has been extensively employed, especially for 2D convolutional neural networks, and has proven surprisingly effective for a variety of different medical tasks [66, 96, 99, 100]. Despite the popularity of this approach, the literature does not provide definitive evidence on whether fine-tuning can offer superior performance with respect to training from scratch, and in which conditions [101]. Due to the difference between the experimental setup, the training set size, the source datasets, and the large variability in medical images appearances and tasks, it is difficult to derive from the current literature consistent indications. Many published works are proofs of concept focusing on specific applications, hence the results are difficult to generalize and, for the time being, it is likely that each new task needs to be individually evaluated.

In general, transfer learning from natural images appears beneficial compared to training from scratch when the training set is small compared to the number of parameters: not only training is faster, but the final performance is higher and the gap increases as the training set size decreases [66, 99, 102]. Tajbakhsh and colleagues addressed four different applications: polyp detection in colonoscopy, image quality assessment in colonoscopy, pulmonary embolism detection in CT, and intima-media boundary segmentation in ultrasonography [100]. Overall, they observed that fine-tuning only the last layers performed worse than full training, but fine-tuning more layers was comparable to, or outperformed full training. Fine-tuning more layers was especially important for polyp detection and intima-media boundary segmentation, which the authors hypothesize are less similar to ImageNet than other applications. On the other hand, in histopathology, where training data is notoriously scarce, partial fine-tuning has proven beneficial compared to fully fine-tuning [103]; for smaller datasets, even off-the-shelf pre-trained features can provide acceptable results, often better than full-training [103, 104]. A few authors have suggested that non-medical datasets that have higher inter-class image similarities, such as Places, may be a better source than ImageNet to highlight fine-grained details in medical images, but their use is still not widespread [96].

The positive effects of transfer learning from the natural domain do not always hold, and there are also counter-examples when transfer learning did not improve the performance [105]. In fact, the considerable differences between medical images and natural scenes image have led many authors to question the ultimate effectiveness of transferring from natural scenes, especially for domains such as CT scans and MRI [55]. Many medical images are grey scale, with more than 255 levels, and shape and textural information is predominant with respect to color. The resolution of medical images is usually much higher than the resolutiuon of natural images, and clinically significant details may be lost at the downsampling factors normally used in computer vision [54]. Natural image classification is unaffected by changes of intensity value so long as the local contrast does not change, whereas in medical images the intensity values recorded are informative of certain classes of pathology and in selected cases may even be standardized (e.g. intensity values in CT scans are measured in Hounsfield units). Much of the effort in training classifiers for natural images goes to discard variability due to occlusions, changes in viewpoint, illumination and so forth, which are fundamentally non-existent in medical images; on the other hand, classifiers in the medical domain must be able to disentangle very subtle class-specific variability from large intra-individual variability.

The impressive results obtained, among others, in head CT classification [55] and mammography classification [54] highlight the feasibility, and possible superiority, of training representations from scratch with annotated training datasets ranging from hundreds of thousands to millions of images. Emerging evidence in literature suggests that, for larger medical datasets containing at least a few hundred thousands samples, transfer learning does not provide much competitive advantage over learning from scratch. However, the reader should be aware that the two strategies are likely to converge to different representations (i.e. features), even when the discriminative performance is similar.

Transfer learning across medical imaging modalities is less investigated due to the lack of publicly available large and diverse medical datasets. Menegola and colleagues compared off-the-shelf feature and fine-tuning strategies for melanoma classification using two datasets for pretraining: Imagenet and the Kaggle Diabetic Retinopathy (KaggleDR) which comprises roughly 35,000 images [102]. While the KaggleDR dataset is supposed to be a closer task, in this case transfer from ImageNet was found to be more successful. It should be noticed however that melanoma detection is one of the few medical images tasks that relies on photos, and hence low level features are likely to be very close to ImageNet; histopathology images are also more similar to natural scenes than, for instance, CT or MRI scans. Another possible explanation is that medical datasets tend to be very specialized on specific tasks, thus resulting in very specialized features; indeed, diversity is an often overlooked factor for successful knowledge transfer [101].

Alternatively, one could resort to a dual transfer strategy, as exemplified in Figure 2.6, in which the network is first fine-tuned on a bridge medical dataset and then on the target dataset; this strategy has so far proven beneficial as long as the bridge dataset contains images from the same modality, but not necessarily the same task, of the target dataset [99,106]. A systematic investigation across a wide variety of tasks and domains, however, is lacking.

Finally, let us consider now which strategies have been tested, so far, to mitigate the differences between the non-medical and medical domain. One strategy is to transform medical images, e.g. through *colorization*, to increase their similarity to natural scene images. For instance, Teare and colleagues used genetic algorithms to discover an optimal set of preprocessing transformations for mammography false color enhancement, and found that they could significantly improve the classification accuracy of a network pre-trained on ImageNet [64]. In the case of CT scans, pseudo-color images can be generated by applying different window/level settings on each channel, similar to the process employed by radiologists to enhance the contrast of different tissues [66].

Besides their distinctive visual appearance, an important limitation in transfer learning from the natural domain is that the available pre-trained architectures have been adapted to (usually low resolution, bidimensional) image analysis. This is a fundamental limitation expecially when dealing with high resolution, volumetric data. Increasing the resolution of feature maps can be achieved by extracting features from lower convolutional layers [101] or removing pooling layers [48]. While techniques such as 2.5D convolutions can effectively bridge between the 3D and 2D representations, it is likely that even greater benefits can be obtained by adopting ad-hoc representations, such as 3D convolutional layers.

2.2.4 Domain Adaptation

Designing machine learning systems which can effectively generalize to different visual domains is an important problem in robotics, artificial vision and of course, medical image analysis [107].

This problem has been studied in several settings in which the most common one assumes that unlabelled data from the target domain is available at training (unsupervised domain adaptation), possibly supplemented by a small sample of labelled target data (supervised or semi-supervised). More recently, researchers have started to tackle the more difficult, but equally compelling scenario, when the tested target domain is not available at training time, usually denoted as *domain generalization* [108]. In the medical

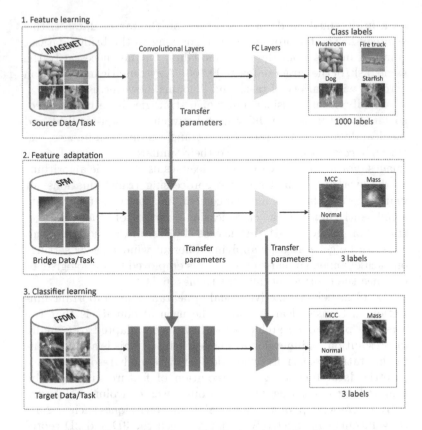

Figure 2.6   In this example, a dual-step transfer learning across different domains and tasks is illustrated. The source task is the ImageNet 1000-classes classification task, trained on a large dataset of roughly 1,000,000 images. The target task is full-field digital mammography (FFDM). An intermediate or bridge dataset, based on Screen-Film mammography (SFM) is used for feature adaptation: alternatively, it is possible to transfer directly from the source to the target task. To transfer across substantially different tasks, the final fully connected layers are stripped and substituted with new layers, which are then trained from random initialization. Convolutional layers parameters are initialized from the source task, and then fine-tuned (light gray) or frozen (dark gray), depending on the size of the training set.

domain, testing on the target domain is technically required for regulatory purposes, but for certain modalities testing all possible variations of acquisition parameters is largely unfeasible and hence robustness to visual domain shift is an important goal for the research community.

Two main strategies are available for domain adaptation in classical ML or deep learning, one based on instance re-weighting and the other on feature alignment. Feature realignment has been used in conjunction with traditional feature extraction techniques e.g. through histogram matching [109]. Algorithm-wise, however, deep learning offers new opportunities for feature re-alignment. On one hand, it is possible to train end-to-end architectures that minimize both a given task, and a domain shift measure. The domain shift is expressed in terms of modeling the difference in the features spaces, or through adversarial domain adaptation techniques [107].

Another direction deals with image (instead of feature) transformation, where the visual domain of the source or target task is modelled so that adaptation happens at the input level and the classification network can be reused without further modification. This approach sometimes offer better interpretability, but does not necessarily lead to the best result. The medical imaging community has long studied image transformations to harmonize medical images across scanners, and patient population: notable examples include normalization of mammographic images across different vendors, normalization of MRI sequence data, artifact removals and de-noising. This work has been facilitated by the ability to model the acquisition process from a physics viewpoint, as well as the relative standardization of image acquisition, which make close world assumptions more realistic than in the general computer vision domain. Such techniques have also been successfully applied as a preprocessing step prior to applying deep learning techniques. To the best of our knowledge, techniques that model the image transformation as part of a deep neural network have been seldom investigated in the medical domain.

When labelled data is available for the target domain, the most common strategy within the medical domain is to employ supervised transfer learning from the source to the target domain, e.g. when applying models trained on different scanners or with different sequences. The related literature has focused on determining the amount of data needed to re-train the network, how deep learning generalizes to different sequences, and on how many layers should be retrained given the amount of available data [99, 110].

This approach has merits but is limited by the availability of labelled samples and of data with sufficient diversity.

A more interesting approach is that of unsupervised domain adaptation. This can be achieved through instance-level transfer, where the source distribution is manipulated to match the target distribution by weighting the instances for training [96]. Notice that the weighting can be derived from the feature distribution, but can also reflect a priori domain knowledge. For instance, when classifying subjects as having Alzheimer's disease, Wachinger and Reuter perform weighting based on patient characteristics such as age, which are not used for classification but are a common source of database bias, especially when the training dataset is not entirely representative of the target clinical population [111].

Unsupervised domain adaptation is particularly appealing for the medical domain where data is often abundant (privacy restrictions aside), but labels are scarce and expensive to acquire. Recently, generative adversarial networks (GANs) have made great achievements in generating realistic images and adversarial learning excels in mapping data distributions for domain adaptation, by learning to generate realistic samples for the target domain. A few applications are already available in the medical domain [74, 112–114]. Most works have focused on medical modalities, such as Magnetic Resonance Imaging, where the number of possible acquisition sequences and parameters is very high, and usually poorly standardized across different institutions. Recent works adopted CycleGANs or similar architectures to train segmentation models when the target domain was completely unlabeled [115–117]. Mahmood and colleagues have used a similar technique to train a network for endoscopy analysis on synthetic data [112]. Often, these methods are augmented with semantic-aware losses to avoid the loss of useful diagnostic feature [94, 113].

2.2.5 Multi-task Learning

Multi-task learning refers to the joint learning of multiple tasks by the same model. By sharing representations between related tasks, we can enable our model to generalize better on each individual task. This approach is particularly effective in computer vision and medical image analysis, where features are often relevant to multiple tasks, and is usually achieved through parameter sharing [96]. Examples include the detection of different types of lesions in images of the same anatomical district [48, 55]. Another possible strategy is using a single network to model different tasks (detection, segmentation and classification) for a single pathology. In most cases, multi-task learning is implemented by sharing the weights or parameters for the model, but using different outputs depending on the task. There are however exceptions to this rule. For instance, Moeskops and colleagues designed a network where multiple tasks (tissue segmentation in MR, pectoral muscle segmentation in MR and coronary artery segmentation in CT) are learned in a joint label space, like they were a single multi-class problem [118]. Alternatively, tasks can be learnt sequentially, rather than in parallel: in this case, some authors have observed benefits in learning easier tasks first, and then proceeding to more complex tasks, much like radiologists are trained [119].

2.2.6 Semi-supervised and Unsupervised Learning

Data starvation is often mentioned as one of the key obstacles to the application of deep learning in radiology [120]. However, this notion is only partially correct [28]. The radiology workflow is mostly digitized, and thousands if not millions of images are stored in picture archiving and communication systems (PACS) worldwide. Other specialties, like ophthalmology and pathology, are catching up. In many cases the challenge is thus the cost of labelling the data. For this reason, researchers have always been interested in designing techniques for unsupervised and semi-supervised learning. We here refer to semi-supervised learning in its broadest sense, as techniques that can learn from partial annotations. Purely unsupervised methods may fail to capture subtle diagnostic features, and hence semi-supervised methods are, in the authors' view, more likely to succeed.

Unsupervised or semi-supervised learning can be used to pretrain a classification model by learning an initial representation from unlabelled data. Among unsupervised methods, generative models like GANs have tremendous potential to uncover representations directly from data. Self-supervised methods are another emerging trend in representation learning. The underlying idea is to assign artificial labels to unlabeled medical images and, through a process known as surrogate supervision, pre-train a deep neural network model for the target medical image analysis task lacking sufficient labeled training data. An example of surrogate task is rotation, where the network is trained to estimate the degree by which an image has been rotated. Such supervisory signal can be automatically generated, and is especially effective for images which present a consistent anatomy and adequate landmarks, such as the heart or the liver. Even if the resulting learned representation is not as effective as the representations learned through strong supervision, it still outperforms random initialization, and may even outperform transfer learning from unrelated domains [121–123].

Relaxing the constraints on annotation, e.g. by learning to learn from noisy labels, is another important direction for semi-superivsed learning. Noisy labels could be harvested from PACS and EHR systems, where a wealth of information is available in the form of free-text reports [124]. Additionally, radiologists routinely record annotations in PACS in the form of bookmarks such as bounding boxes, arrows, lines or lesions measurements [48,120,125]. We expect research in optimally leveraging free-text and structured reports for network training to increase in the near future.

While such annotations may be noisier than those collected specifically for research purposes, it has to be noticed however that radiological features are inherently ambiguous, and radiologists' reports are not definitive expressions of ground truth [120,126]. For the same lesion or case, there may be significant inter-rater variability in the rating or segmentation provided by different radiologists, that have often prompted researchers to collect annotations from large panels of expert radiologists [127,128]. At the time of writing, designing robust training algorithms in the presence of labelling noise is an active area of research, and one that is particularly relevant to the medical domain. There is however promising empirical evidence that deep neural networks, despite their high model capacity which in principle enables them to memorize noisy labels, may in practice be robust to a moderate amount of labeling noise, particularly when leveraging a large scale training set.

Another flourishing line of research leverages patient-level annotations to train lesion-level classifiers. In this setting, we know that an abnormality is present in an image, but its precise location is unknown, yet we wish to predict it. In machine learning, this setting is known as multiple-instance learning (MIL), in which the learner receives a set of labeled bags, each containing many (unlabelled) instances. In the simplest case of binary classification, a bag is labeled positive if it contains at least one positive instance. MIL is a natural learning scenario for medical image analysis because labels are often not available at the desired granularity. And has been applied to several application domains including histopathology analysis, diabetic retinopathy, and lesion detection in lung, abdomen and breast images [96].

In the next chapter, we will see how architectural choices, quantity and quantity of the training data and selected training strategies may affect performance in exemplifying cases.

CHAPTER 3

Applying AI in Medical Imaging

Since medical images were made available in digital format, initially through digitalization of screen films and later through direct digital acquisition, computerized image processing and visualization techniques have been used to achieve more accurate, reliable and faster image interpretation. Practical applications, however, have evolved following advances in computer science and machine learning, on the one hand, and of the underlying imaging technologies, on the other hand. In this chapter, we will follow this evolution by presenting the plethora of AI practical applications in medical imaging, and finally delve into the details of exemplifying case studies.

3.1 FROM EXPERT SYSTEMS TO DEEP LEARNING: HISTORICAL PERSPECTIVE

Computerized medical image interpretation dates back to the 1960's, although the field gained much momentum in the 1990's [129, 130]. While the dominant field is undoubtedly radiology, medical image analysis has found applications in many fields of medicine, including digital pathology [103, 131–133], ophthalmology [134–136], dermatology [137–139] and endoscopy [100, 140]. The reader will indulge us if, out of habit, we refer mostly to radiology, but our considerations apply almost *verbatim* to other fields as well.

From an historical perspective, three periods can be identified in the evolution of medical image interpretation [141]. Early days were dominated by *expert systems*, and especially rule-based reasoning systems. In the radiological domain, such rule systems were usually applied to imaging features extracted through image processing techniques. However, over time this approach proved to be very brittle in solving perception tasks across all spectra of inputs, from images to speech and text, mostly due to the inherent ambiguity of perceptual stimuli.

The 1990's saw the emergence of Computer Aided Diagnosis (CAD) and quantitative image analysis tools. Generally speaking, the terms computer aided detection and diagnosis denote a broad range of artificial intelligence (AI) software designed to help radiologists improve their diagnostic accuracy. These use cases, along with their fundamental building blocks, are illustrated in Section 3.2.2. From a technical point of view, the majority of solutions in this period were based on pattern recognition or classification, image segmentation techniques, or probabilistic methods. The interested reader is referred to Chapter 1 for an overview of traditional pattern recognition technique.

Many excellent resources provide an illustration of the technical foundations of image processing techniques [142, 143], and their applications in the biomedical domain [144]. Techniques in this domain usually fall under various categories: image enhancement, segmentation, registration or visualization techniques. Their application usually requires strong background knowledge about the underlying anatomy, as well as the physical process of image formation. Probabilistic models are also inspired by the human decisional chain, but enriched with a probabilistic perspective. In this type of technique, the underlying model is still derived from human expertise, but its parameters are computed from a labelled reference dataset through probabilistic methods that determine the most likely solutions [145]. Examples of such methods include atlas-based segmentation techniques [145], and probabilistic segmentation models [146]. As an example, probabilistic methods have found many applications in brain imaging, where the position of brain structures is relatively stable and thus strong prior probabilities are available [147].

In recent years, the use of deep learning has become pervasive in most perception and reasoning tasks. The turning point for the computer vision community was in 2012, when a convolutional neural network called AlexNet won the ImageNet Large

Scale Image Recognition challenge by a large margin [91]. In the medical imaging domain, the transition gradually started a few years later, as the technology became more mature, and skyrocketed in 2015: in a survey of the literature conducted in 2017, more than 300 articles were cataloged, of which more than 200 were published in 2016 alone [28]. The first deep learning-based application was cleared by the FDA in 2017.

Applying deep learning to medical imaging poses several technical challenges, which are partly reviewed in Chapter 2 of this book and in the case studies in the present chapter.

The availability of deep learning has changed the medical imaging landscape by enabling learning directly from data through general purpose learning algorithms. This shift, from engineering to learning from data, has significantly reduced the time needed to develop new applications. It must be noticed in the medical domain, conventional image processing, feature extraction and AI/ML approaches still co-exist to a large extent; in many cases the best performing deep learning methods incorporate task-specific knowledge or augment convolutional neural networks using novel data processing or augmentation techniques [28].

Deep learning has consistently achieved state-of-the-art results in several medical imaging applications [28]. In selected cases, these methodologies have reached or even surpassed human-level performance. Examples include detection of pneumonia in chest X-ray [57, 148], skin cancer classification in dermatology [137, 138], radiograph interpretation [56, 149], pathology detection in head CT images [55, 150], diagnosis of diabetic retinopathy [151], and mammographic analysis [152, 153]. These findings, while certainly exciting, need to be interpreted with care, as medical interpretation entails more than pure pattern recognition. In many cases, comparison is performed on a subset of all possible tasks [138], and excludes information normally available during clinical practice, such as anamnesis, patient history, and prior scans [148]. Nonetheless, it is evident that at least part of the radiologic workflow is amenable to automation, and that such evolution is within the grasp of current technology [154, 155].

High-profile success cases have stimulated investments resulting not only in the birth of many dedicated start-ups, but also in several of the world IT giants entering the market alongside traditional players in the biomedical field [156].

Technology evolves along a continuum, and many applications which are now called Artificial Intelligence were previously

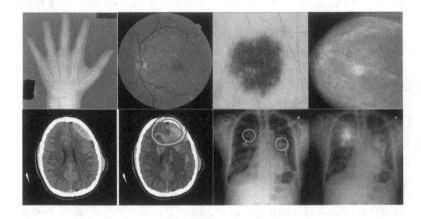

Figure 3.1 Examples of diagnostic tasks where AI has matched or surpassed the average performance of human readers. Top row (left to right): assessment of skeletal maturity on pediatric hand radiographs [157], diagnostic of diabetic retinopathy [158], lesion detection in dermoscopy images [159], mammography diagnosis [160]. Bottom row (left to right): head CT analysis [55], chest X-ray diagnosis [148]. Images with superimposed heatmaps allow us to interpret the network prediction and verify that the abnormality was correctly localized.

known under other names, such as CAD systems. Following the so-called "AI Winter" of the late 1980's and early 1990's, the use of the artificial intelligence term declined as new terminology was adopted. Nowadays, the keywords AI and ML are widely used, and have come to denote a wide range of applications. We prefer here to adopt a categorization which follows the intended clinical use, rather than the implementing technology. Many long-standing challenges related to the implementation and clinical validation of CAD systems remain unchanged, regardless of the underlying technology.

Notwithstanding, marked improvements in performance do open new perspectives in terms of clinical applications, especially for triage applications [150, 152, 161]. At the time of writing, the notion of an algorithm performing an independent diagnosis opens medico-legal issues that are yet to be solved [154], and are certainly beyond the scope of this book.

Advances in machine learning also bring the promise of autonomous systems that can learn and evolve in a (mostly) unsupervised fashion [154]. Current implementations of deep learning trained in a supervised fashion on massive, high quality, curated training sets are often specific to a given pathology or application. They are deployed as static, "locked" systems that, like their CAD counterparts, can be updated but do not learn automatically. In the upcoming years, we envision an increased interest in researching continual and lifelong learning algorithms suited to the needs of the medical domain [162]. This issue will be explained in Chapter 4 from a regulatory perspective.

3.2   USE CASES: PAST, PRESENT AND FUTURE

3.2.1   Quantitative Image Analysis

Quantitative Image Analysis (QIA) refers to the extraction of quantifiable features from medical images for the assessment of the presence, severity, degree of change, or status of a disease, injury, or chronic condition, compared to the normal, healthy status. The extraction of quantitative data is crucial to fully exploit the value of medical images, going beyond the visual appearance, and hence the "picture" [163]. Furthermore, quantitative analysis has the potential to extract information which is not visible to the human eye, yet has prognostic and diagnostic value.

QIA encompasses a broad range of applications, one of the earliest being the measurement of shape and volume of organs, tissues and lesions. Manual segmentation is extremely time consuming and hence its use in clinical practice is rare. When possible, linear measurements such as in the RECIST criteria, are adopted instead. However, volumetric measurement, based on precise segmentation techniques, provides additional and often more accurate assessment that can be used for diagnosis, risk assessment and monitoring of disease [164, 165]. Volumetric applications are also important in the assessment of organ functionality, for instance in cardiology and brain imaging. An example is the segmentation and measurement of the carotid intima-media, discussed in Section 3.3.1. Deep learning based methods have been applied to the segmentation of several organs and sub-structures including abdominal organs (e.g., kidney, bladder, livery, pancreas and prostate), visceral fat, brain images, fibroglandular tissue in breast images, heart, lungs and bones (e.g. knees, spine) [32].

Functional and nuclear imaging is also particularly amenable to quantitative image analysis [166]. Starting from the segmentation of an organ or lesion of interest, metabolic and molecular information can be measured and quantified, as opposed to merely visualized and qualitatively assessed. One of the goals of QIA is the identification of quantitative imaging biomarkers. The Quantitative Imaging Biomarkers Alliance (QIBA), organized by the Radiological Society of North America (RSNA), has formally defined a QI biomarker as "an objective characteristic derived from an in vivo image measured on a ratio or interval scale as indicators [sic] of normal biological processes, pathogenic processes, or a response to a therapeutic intervention." [167] This strict definition is meant to guide research toward biomarkers that may be assessed and compared with robust statistical calculations including frequency distributions, medians, means, standard deviations, and standard errors of the mean.

From an image processing point of view, research and deployment focuses on segmentation techniques, on one hand, and on feature extraction, on the other hand. While QIA poses much emphasis on standardization and reproducibility, a high quality segmentation is crucial, and hence a manual correction step is often foreseen. Accurate display, integration and standardized reporting are also crucial for translation in clinical practice [168].

3.2.2 Computer Aided Detection and Diagnosis

Human error is an inevitable part of medicine, and radiology is no exception. Diagnostic errors are the most common source of errors in diagnostic radiology, accounting for nearly 75% of all medical malpractice claims against radiologists [169]. Furthermore, radiological features are inherently ambiguous, and significant interrater variability is often observed in detection or characterization of lesion patterns; hence, a certain rate of misclassification may be inherent in the diagnostic process [120, 126–128].

In the early literature, misdiagnosis was attributed either to fatigue and perceptual oversight (i.e. the abnormality is visible but not seen by the radiologist at the time of reading), or interpretation errors (i.e. the abnormality is perceived but incorrectly dismissed as a benign finding). Cognitive biases such as "satisfaction of search", the phenomenon whereby detection of one abnormality results in a premature termination of the search, could also potentially result in misdiagnosis. More recently, a steady increase in radiologists' workload, as well as in the volume and complexity of three-dimensional images, has also stimulated research on how to speed up the interpretation process and reduce variability among readers.

The acronym CAD has therefore come to denote a broad class of image processing and AI/ML software, whose purpose can be either (i) to identify potential lesions and bring them to the attention of the radiologist (Computer Aided Detection or CADe), or (ii) to estimate the likelihood that an abnormality represents an actual disease process based on image-extracted features (Computer Aided Diagnosis or CADx), and help the radiologist make an informed decision. Compared to many computer vision applications, CAD software combines with human interpretation to reach a final diagnosis.

Starting from initial experiments with mammography in the 1980's, the field of computer aided detection and diagnosis has rapidly grown to a mature field with several commercial systems available and an expanding body of clinical evidence. CAD applications have been developed for a multitude of imaging technologies and clinical applications [170].

The most diffuse CAD applications are related to cancer detection and diagnosis. Cancer screening is particularly amenable to automation: on one hand the task of detecting a narrow range of possible abnormalities within specific organs is relatively easy to automate for computer vision scientists and engineers, while on the other hand, the need to search for a small number of lesions in large volumes of asymptomatic subjects is a repetitive, yet difficult and error-prone task for the radiologist. In 2011, van Ginneken et al. published a list of CAD systems that had received clearance from the US Food and Drug Administration at the time: 15 out of 16 systems targeted cancerous or pre-cancerous lesions in CT colonography, mammography, chest radiographs or CT scans [130]. Other interesting applications can be found in cardiology, neurology, ophthalmology and for the detection of non-cancerous abnormalities, such as interstitial lung disease or pulmonary embolism [28, 170–174]. Case studies related to mammography, CT colonography and diabetic retinopathy are illustrated in Sections 3.3.3, 3.3.2 and 3.3.4.

For many years, CAD applications were implemented through a pipeline of image processing and pattern recognition modules, as defined in Chapter 1, and illustrated in Figure 1.1. First, images are preprocessed to enhance quality, and then the organ of interest is segmented; secondly, initial candidates are identified by applying pattern recognition techniques, yielding a list of potential abnormalities or lesion candidates. Segmentation algorithms may be employed to obtain a more precise outline of each potential abnormality. Finally, a further classification step is applied to reduce the number of false positive candidates. CADx systems will also include a classification step designed to provide the clinician with an assessment of disease, disease type, severity, stage, progression or regression [175].

Feature extraction is a key component of both CADe and CADx. The reader is referred to Chapter 1 for a description and taxonomy of traditional feature extraction methods. It should be noticed however that some applications may also require extracting features from 4D datasets, where the fourth dimension is time. This is true for example in functional imaging, which detects or measures changes in metabolism, blood flow, or chemical composition through the administration of markers or contrast agents, or by employing ad hoc imaging sequences. This introduces new classes of spatio-temporal features, which are tied to the temporal properties of the functional signal (kinetics) and to the spatial distribution of temporal changes (spatio-temporal features). Figure 3.2 illustrates 4D feature extraction.

These broad operational principles are shared by most CAD applications, and essentially all oncology applications, but specific

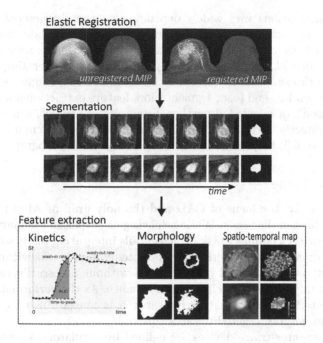

Figure 3.2   Spatio-temporal feature extraction from dynamic-contrast enhanced breast MRI. In DCE-MRI, multiple sequences are acquired after injection of a paramagnetic contrast agent. Signal intensity reflects the properties of the local vasculature, which in turns reflects metabolic and tumoral activity. First, the temporal sequences needs to be re-aligned to correct for movements which may mask or simulate the presence of lesions, as evident from the Maximum Intensity Projection maps. Then, the contrast-enhanced lesion is segmented for subsequent feature extraction. Specific classes of features relevant to 4D image data include lesion kinetics, morphology and spatio-temporal features. Figure partially adapted from Agliozzo, S., et al. "Computer-aided diagnosis for dynamic contrast-enhanced breast MRI of mass-like lesions using a multiparametric model combining a selection of morphological, kinetic, and spatiotemporal features." *Medical Physics* 39.4 (2012): 1704–1715.

implementations vary widely depending on the characteristics of the organ, lesion type, and imaging modality, and last but not least, whether the implementation is based on deep learning. The latter, in fact, has not necessarily changed but rather simplified this workflow, as many steps may be combined in a single network trained end-to-end (e.g., segmentation, feature extraction and classification), or avoided altogether. Examples of how DL can be applied directly to the input image, without the need for a multi-stage pipeline, will be provided in the case study of mammography.

3.2.3 Triage

Historically, the focus of CAD and the holy grail of AI is to improve human diagnosis. While achieving or surpassing human performance is a complex task, which entails integrating many sources of information and experience, undoubtedly many tasks within the current workflow could be automated without necessarily targeting an improvement in clinical performance. As the performance of computerized image analysis increases, it is conceivable that more devices will be targeted towards this end.

Computer-triage devices are defined by regulatory agencies as "computerized systems intended to, in any way, reduce or eliminate any aspect of clinical care currently provided by a clinician". This would be particularly useful in a high-volume screening setting, where a CAD triage could be used to quickly identify normal patients, leaving abnormal ones for radiologists [152, 165, 176]. Other typical settings are those when timely response is needed, as in emergency care, and/or a doctor may not be readily available, as in low-income countries and point-of-care scenarios [150].

The concept of triage can be extended to include systems which, for example, prioritize reporting queues, by automatically selecting the findings in need of faster action.

3.2.4 Image Registration

Registration involves estimating the spatial transformation between pixels in two images that we wish to align. It allows us to combine images from different modalities and/or to align images from different patients to a common atlas [177]; it also allows us to align temporal sequences of images [178] and therein compensate motion artifacts [179]. Registration can be used to improve the visualization of medical images, but it is also used as a preprocessing step in CAD, radiomics or QIA to suppress the effect of patient movement on feature extraction, as exemplified in Figure 3.2.

Registration is solved by finding the optimal transformation between the input (moving) and the output (target) coordinate space that maximizes some measure of image similarity between the target image and the (warped) moving image. Since the optimal transformation needs to be calculated for each image pair, the process can be quite slow. A large variety of registration methods have been proposed in literature, which differ in the nature of the transformation (rigid, affine, elastic, curve), the domain of the transformation (global, local), the degree of interaction (interactive, semi-automatic, automatic) and the optimization procedure or algorithm; the interested reader is referred to the many books and reviews published on the subject [177, 180, 181].

Deep learning has also been applied to the task of image registration, but the literature on the topic is still remarkably new and far from clinical applications. A possible approach to non-rigid registration involves designing a neural network that estimates a pixel-wise deformation field from pairs of images, where one image is the fixed image and the second is the moving image [182, 183]. Let us recall that a neural network is, first and foremost, a method to approximate any function, and this extends beyond learning classification functions. In this case, the network is used to approximate the deformation field, i.e. a spatial transformation that establishes pixel or voxel-wise spatial correspondence between the two images; the moving image is then warped to realign it with the target image. The current literature suggests that the CNN-based approach could be computationally faster at test time, albeit slightly less accurate, than traditional registration technique; this however, may change as new methods are proposed.

3.2.5 Radiomics: Radiology Meets Big Data

The concept that biomedical images contain information that reflects the underlying pathophysiology, and that these relationships can be revealed via quantitative image analyses, motivates the development of the growing radiomics field. Radiomics entails the conversion of digital medical images into mineable high-dimensional data through the process of segmentation and feature extraction. Radiomics was first formally introduced by Lambin and colleagues in 2012 [184]. According to the seminal review by Gillies et al.,

"The radiomics process is designed to extract a large number of quantitative features from digital images, place these data in shared databases along with other relevant patient characteristics including genomic data, and subsequently mine the data for hypothesis generation, testing, or both". While radiomics primarily grew out of basic research, as a technique for exploratory data analysis and hypothesis generation, clinical applications have started to emerge, mostly related to building diagnostic and prognostic models, assessing tumor aggressiveness, and evaluating treatment plans.

The radiomics workflow involves the acquisition of anatomical, functional and metabolic imaging, the segmentation of organs or lesions using automatic or semi-automatic techniques, and the extraction of multiple types of features. Although semantic features are commonly used by radiologists to describe lesions, their descriptive, qualitative and subjective nature allow for a crude representation of the underlying biology. On the contrary, quantitative descriptors can be locally derived by computing first-, second- or higher-order statistics from individual image regions. While radiomics features can be extracted both through traditional feature extraction or DL methods, at the present the former is predominant in the literature, especially textural features [3]. This is certainly due to their greater potential for standardization and simplicity of extraction. Up to 700 different features have been extracted from a single image region, yielding a tremendous amount of information. For a technical description of feature extraction and selection methods, the reader is referred to Chapter 1. Techniques derived from machine learning, data analytics and bioinformatics are then used for data mining and for building diagnostic and prognostic models. A number of libraries and toolkits are now available to implement radiomics pipelines; an illustrative example is provided in Figure 3.3.

Radiomics stems directly from the field of quantitative image analysis, and shares many similarities with CAD applications as well, expecially CADx. The discriminating line is often blurred in the relevant literature, largely reflecting the evolution (and hype) in terminology. The radiomics term has become synonymous with the feature extraction term both in the literature and by extension to CADx applications.

Radiomics, QIA and CAD rely on similar intermediate steps, such as lesion segmentation (although radiomics may employ manual or semi-automatic segmentation to maximize accuracy) and feature extraction. Unlike CAD though, the radiomics process is not (necessarily) tied to a precise diagnostic task. Similarly to quantitative image analysis, much emphasis is posed on the reproducibility and repeatibility of the feature extraction process [185].

Similarly to CAD, radiomics have seen the most important developments in oncology applications. One of the more interesting and novel aspects of radiomics is that quantitative image features offer distinctive information on tumor phenotype and microenvironment (or habitat). Such information, currently underutilized, could provide information that is correlated to genomic and proteomics patterns. Furthermore, radiomics can be linked with the concept of radio-genomics, which assumes that imaging features are related to gene signatures [184, 186]. This hypothesis, which was postulated in the seminal work by Lambin and collagues, is increasingly supported by experimental evidence. For instance, Kuo and colleagues identified hepatocellular carcinoma imaging phenotypes that correlated with a doxorubicin drug response gene expression program [187], suggesting that radio-genomic analyses could be used to guide the selection of therapy for individual tumors [188].

A major strength of the radiomics approach is the possibility to measure and visualize tumor heterogeneity; most clinically relevant solid tumors are highly heterogeneous at the phenotypic, physiological, and genomic levels, and genomic heterogeneity within tumors and across metastatic tumor sites in the same patient is a major cause of treatment failure and emergence of therapy resistance. A thorough discussion of the connections with genomics is, however, beyond the scope of this book, which will focus solely on the imaging and data analysis aspects of the radiomics workflow.

3.2.6 Applications beyond Image Interpretation

Applications of AI in medical imaging are not limited to image interpretation, and in fact other applications which do not entail rigorous and costly validation studies may find their way into the clinical environment quite soon [165, 190].

Deep learning has been applied to improve the quality of reconstructed images, including image enhancement, noise reduction, artifact reduction and reconstruction [32]. In these cases, the output of the ML algorithm is an image (or a transformation of) with improved quality over traditional image processing methods.

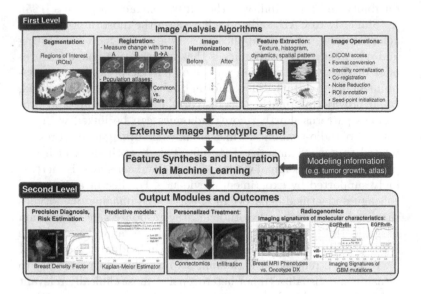

Figure 3.3   Overview of the radiomics analysis cycle as implemented in the Cancer Imaging Phenomics toolkit (CaPTk). At the first level, CaPTk provides image preprocessing and feature extraction functions that can be used to generate an extensive panel of features ranging from segmentation of tumors and its partitions, to extraction of textural and perfusion dynamic features, and many others. At the second level, these features and maps are integrated into diagnostic and predictive models, e.g. for prediction of clinical outcome, and estimation of molecular characteristics of tumors. Figure reproduced with permission from Davatzikos, Christos, et al. "Cancer imaging phenomics toolkit: quantitative imaging analytics for precision diagnostics and predictive modeling of clinical outcome." *Journal of Medical Imaging* 5.1 (2018) [189].

Another emerging area of application is related to the management and optimization of the radiology workflow, starting from exam scheduling and resource optimization. Diagnosis and reporting can be made more efficient by prioritizing exams based on potential findings, by displaying and aggregating information from images and electronic medical records, and by providing tools such as speech recognition and image-to-text tools for reporting. Medical associations and healthcare providers are also incentivizing the use of decision support systems to reduce inappropriate ordering of high cost imaging scans.

Quality assurance and management can also benefit from the current surge in AI. For instance, AI-based image analysis tools may be used for internal peer-review of reports. Quality management, however, extends beyond reporting, including image quality, radiation dose, scan time, patient positioning and other aspects of technologist's performance, up to the evaluation and creation of new study protocols. As an example, ML-based tools have been developed to automate assessment of adequate breast positioning in mammography, as a more systematic and cost-effective alternative to visual assessment.

Last but not least, content based-image image retrieval (CBIR) is another important area of research in the medical imaging domain [191]. It entails finding similar images in PACS based not only on specific keywords or imaging parameters, but mostly on the image features, by evaluating similarity with a query image. CBIR systems have also been used as a decision support tool and may complement traditional lesion classification and/or detection approaches.

3.2.7 Applications beyond Radiology: Histopathology

Researchers both in the image analysis and pathology fields have long recognized the importance of quantitative analysis of pathology images. The benefits would extend beyond clinical benefits, namely a more reproducible and faster diagnosis, to research applications that shed light onto the biological mechanisms of the disease process.

Pathology diagnosis is usually performed by a human pathologist observing the stained specimen on the slide glass using a microscope. In recent years, many acquisition systems have enabled us to capture the entire slide with a scanner and save it as a digital image (whole slide image, WSI), which can be anayzed through digital imaging techniques [28, 192, 193].

CAD in histopathology shares many similarities and challenges with radiology, but it has articulated as a separate field due to the strong peculiarities of histopathology images. For instance, the sheer volume of histopathology data requires dedicated approaches. To give a numerical example, a single core of prostate biopsy tissue digitized at 40× resolution is approximately 15,000 × 15,000 elements or ∼225 million pixels, and a single prostate biopsy procedure can comprise anywhere between 12 to 20 biopsy samples or approximately 2.5 to 4 billion pixels of data generated per patient study, which is roughly 30× times larger than a CT scan. Histological CAD systems often need to process color images and, with the advent of multi-spectral and hyper-spectral imaging, each pixel in a histopathology section could potentially be associated with several hundreds sub-bands and wavelengths [192]. Finally, histopathology image analysis has a strong multi-resolution component. Pathologists acquire different kinds of information from the cellular level to the tissue level by changing the magnifications of a microscope, and different levels of magnification result in different levels of information [193].

The main steps involved in histopathology images analysis are *stain normalization, cellular structures detection, tumor detection, quantitative feature extraction* and development of *classification or prediction models*. Such steps are usually performed on local patches, and then are combined for whole-slide inference depending on the specific pathology or task.

The normalization of the color appearance (stain normalization) plays a crucial role both in the diagnostic field and in the development of automated solutions for quantitative analysis, compensating for variation in the staining and acquisition process [192].

The detection of cellular structure can be applied to identify from macrostructures (steatosis, glands) to cellular and subcellular elements (membranes, nuclei, nucleoli). Then, tumor detection can be performed by classifying such structures (e.g. cell nuclei) into normal or abnormal tissue [133]. An example of histopathology image analysis, as implemented by the AEQUIP (Automated Enhanced QUantitative imaging in Immunohistochemistry and Pathology) system [132, 133], is presented in Figure 3.4.

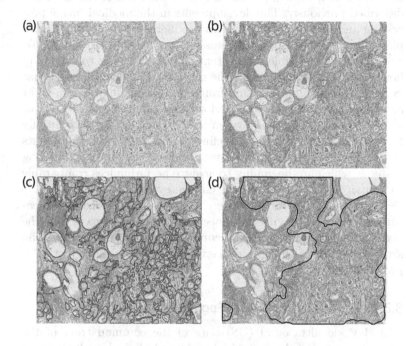

Figure 3.4 Results of the AEQUIP tool applied to prostate cancer detection. The system can automatically extract all the relevant cellular structures ranging from macrostructures (steatosis, glands) to cellular and sub-cellular elements, from images acquired from different tissues (colon, liver, prostate, bone, adrenal glands and thyroid) and magnifications (10×, 20×, 40×). Then it automatically detects cancer tissue within the histological specimens using several computer vision strategies. (a) original image with low stain intensity. (b) image after stain normalization. (c) prostate glands segmentation (black). (d) tumor areas detection (black). Image courtesy of Massimo Salvi and Filippo Molinari, Politecnico di Torino.

3.3   CASE STUDIES

In this section, we will present a few case studies of the use cases described previously. The developments in the medical image processing and interpretation domain are incredibly vast and a complete survey of the applications is out of the scope of this book, and perhaps impossible. Our intention here is rather to exemplify how the design of systems for the support of clinical diagnosis has evolved through time, starting from applications mainly aiming at assisting the clinician in the performance of simple tasks such as measurements. Then we move on to CAD systems, which initially incorporated fairly complex pipelines in order to assist radiologists in the diagnosis, arriving to current state of the art deep learning systems, which are beginning to achieve performances comparable to human experts in standalone clinical evaluation.

We may occasionally refer here to diagnostic performance measures such as sensitivity and specificity, or ROC curves and the corresponding areas under the curve (AUC); for the readers who are not familiar with these concepts, an extensive introduction is provided in Chapter 4.

3.3.1   Carotid Intima-Media Segmentation

The B-Mode ultrasound (US) scan of the common tract of the carotid artery (CCA) is a widely adopted clinical evaluation for the assessment of cardiovascular pathology. Morphological changes, such as plaques or stenosis, are potentially conducive to acute cardiovascular events and an increased thickness of the CCA wall is an important index of progression of atherosclerosis. Specifically, the thickness of the intima-media layers of the carotid wall (referenced in literature as intima-media thickness, IMT) has been tied to the risk of myocardial infarction and stroke. The measurement is typically performed on the distal wall, as this reduces the measurement error [194].

Reproducibility of measurements is key in order for an index to serve as a robust prognostic factor, while studies in literature reported inter- and intra-observer coefficients of variation of around 10% [195], and the possibility of increasing time efficiency by reducing operator intervention is always important, so around the

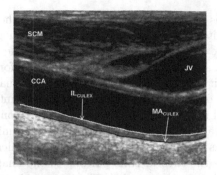

Figure 3.5 Automated segmentation of the carotid intima-media. The lumen-intima and media-adventitia boundaries identified by the automated system are traced in white and black respectively. Figure reprinted with permission from Delsanto et al., "Characterization of a completely user-independent algorithm for carotid artery segmentation in 2-d ultrasound images." *IEEE Transactions on Instrumentation and Measurement*, 56(4):1265–1274, 2007 [199].

year 2000 several approaches for assisting the clinician in measuring the IMT were developed. In the first studies, a certain level of user interaction was required, for example by requiring the user to select the region of interest or provide the coordinates of points belonging to the carotid lumen ([196–198], but around 2005-2006 completely automatic methods were proposed [199].

In the cited work, the measurement of the IMT was substantially reconducted to the problem of segmenting the intima-media layers of the carotid artery. This was achieved through two steps: initially the region of interest (ROI) corresponding to the area of the image portraying the carotid artery was automatically identified, then afterwards the segmentation proper of the intimal and medial layers of the carotid artery wall was performed, isolating them from the third layer of the artery, the adventitia, and from the artery lumen. The identification of the ROI is an important step in the procedure, because it greatly simplifies the segmentation step, as image elements which present confounding features are excluded. ROI identification also facilitates the parametrization of the segmentation steps. In fact, the determination of one or more regions of interest is very often one of the first steps of classical computer vision algorithms in medical imaging.

In the work described, the identification of the ROI was performed with an approach based on an elementary form of ray casting and intensity feature analysis. In fact, combinations of these two techniques often allow to identify portions of interest of medical images, and have been used for example in colon segmentation in CT colonography images [200] and other anatomical structures such as kidneys or aortic aneurisms [201]. Specifically, as in US B-mode images the carotid runs parallel to the image border, the image was analyzed column-wise. The inner and outer adventitial layers were then identified as the two maxima of the intensity profile of each image column, which included in between image pixels presenting features of low intensity mean and variance, as measured on a 20×20 neighborhood, compatible with pixels belonging to the carotid lumen. A low pass filter was also applied prior to this step in order to reduce image noise, again a common procedure in this kind of application.

Once the region of interest is determined, the intima-media layer must be segmented, as illustrated in Figure 3.5. As the intimal and medial layers are separated from the lumen and the adventitia by an interface which is relatively simple, boundary detection techniques (as opposed to other classification techniques such as clustering) may be applied. In the cited paper, an initial estimate places the lumen-intima and the media-adventitia interfaces in correspondence to the maxima of the vertical gradient within the region of interest. This segmentation is then refined through an application of an active contour, also called snake. Active contours are contour-extraction techniques which are based on the minimization of the energy of the contour, given by two components, i.e. the internal energy, which is minimized when smoothing the contour, and the external energy, with the effect of driving the contour towards the object boundaries.

The algorithm in the described work was relatively simple and the medical AI field was still young, yet it yielded a segmentation that was not significantly different than that of the trained manual operator on 116 out of 120 images (in 4 cases ROI identification failed). Technology has since improved, and very recently a deep learning implementation has been proposed [202]. This case study however may serve as an example of how the first applications employed computer vision and feature extraction techniques to provide support to clinicians.

3.3.2 CAD in CT Colonography

Bowel cancer is the third most common cancer worldwide and among the first causes of death by cancer. It is also one of the diseases for which screening has been proven to be most effective, with conclusive evidence that screening reduces mortality. One of the underlying reasons is that, in most cases, colorectal cancer development is slow. A large percentage of colorectal cancers start as benign colorectal adenomas, and estimates of the progression from adenoma to carcinoma are of around 5–10 years. Screening allows the identification of lesions when still at the precancerous stage and thus may in fact prevent the disease altogether. It also allows identifying cancers at the earliest stages in which they are more treatable.

CT colonography is a radiological technique proposed in the mid-1990's as a possible alternative to existing methods such as optical colonoscopy or stool-based tests for the identification of precancerous and cancerous lesions of the colon. It consists in the acquisition of a CT scan of the abdomen, after having properly distended the colon through insufflation of carbon dioxide or air. As residue within the bowel has the same attenuation as the colonic wall, subjects must undergo a specific preparation prior to executing the exam, typically constituted by a low residue diet and the administration of a iodine- and/or barium- based oral contrast agent before the exam. Clinicians may examine the cases either by reading the 2D axial images or by performing a virtual navigation of a 3D reconstruction of the colon.

The peak of popularity enjoyed around 2005 both by CT colonography and computer aided detection systems, the potential of a mass screening application and the relative homogeneity of the pathology represented (in contrast to other organs, significant colorectal pathologies other than polyps and cancer are relatively uncommon, especially in cases indicated for radiological imaging) probably explain the many developments, both commercial and academic, in the field of CT colonography CAD. The CAD systems developed were typically CADe systems, with the aim of detecting colorectal polyps above 6 mm, which are more clinically relevant.

In a typical CT colonography CAD pipeline, the image is first preprocessed by segmenting the colon and performing the so-called *digital cleansing*. The fecal residues, tagged by the oral contrast agents, are segmented, and their intensity values are remapped to the intensity values of air or colon wall, to simulate the appearance of the colon lumen filled with air. After the electronic subtraction of residue, the colon surface is extracted and candidate lesions belonging to the colonic wall are identified. Finally, one or more classifiers filter candidate polyps in order to improve the final false positive rate.

Colon segmentation typically is driven by the identification of the air within the bowel, whose low intensity values are markedly different from those of tissue. The air within the colon must however be distinguished from the external air, the air within the stomach and the air within the lungs. This is typically achieved through a combination of heuristic anatomical considerations (such as the observation that the lungs are typically located in the first 25 mm of the scan), a combination of adaptive region growing and ray casting techniques and in some cases a specific classification step (as for example in the case of the stomach, which may be distinguished due to the ruggedness of the internal wall, which translates into the presentation of specific feature values) [200].

One of the most challenging steps of the CT colonography pipeline is the digital cleansing challenging procedure, especially the process of remapping the colonic wall to non tagged values. This is due to the fact that pseudo-enhancement in the colonic mucosa, which may occur when the colonic wall is submerged in tagged fluid, artificially alters the attenuation value of voxels due to partial volume and acquisition artifacts. Dishomogeneities in tagging are furthermore quite common, hence it may be quite difficult to distinguish between tagged material and adjacent structures with varying levels of pseudo-enhancement. Again, this problem has been solved by applying a combination of ray-casting and region growing techniques. Tagging dishomogeneities may be managed by a local choice of thresholds that vary throughout the colon in order to account for variations in the level of intensity of the marked fluid [203], which may be particularly elevated in the case of same day administration of oral contrast agent. The remapping of the colon wall may then be performed through models which incorporate information of the intensity distribution encountered when passing from the lumen air to the colonic wall.

Once the electronic subtraction of the fecal residue is concluded and the reconstruction and segmentation of the colonic wall has been performed, the CAD system examines voxels of the colonic mucosa to search for polyps. This is typically achieved in two steps: in the first step, i.e. in polyp candidate segmentation, potentially suspicious areas are identified: the goal is to have the highest possi-

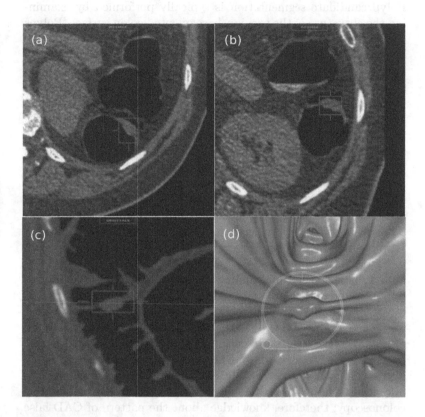

Figure 3.6 A cigar-like polyp of the descending colon. The lesion was missed by the radiologist but was detected by CAD on both the prone (a) and supine (b) acquisitions. Multiplanar reconstruction in sagittal view is shown in (c), whereas the endoluminal view reconstructed via volume rendering by a commercial software is shown in (d). Reproduced with permission from Morra et al., "Computer-aided diagnosis for X-ray imaging," in *Handbook of X-Ray Imaging: Physics and Technology* [204].

ble sensitivity. In the second step, the lesion candidates are filtered to reduce the number of false positives presented by the system. Polyp candidate segmentation is typically performed by examining the curvature of the previously segmented colon surface. Polyps can in fact be generally modeled as semi-spheres protruding into the colon lumen. Two curvature features which have been well described in literature for polyp candidate segmentation and classification are *shape index* and *curvedness*. These geometrical descriptors may be computed as the first and second order derivatives in intensity level differentiation and express the local shape and the magnitude of the curvature. Shape index and curvedness can quite accurately distinguish polyps from other colonic structures, such as folds, which have a "ridge"-like shape and larger curvature values [203, 205]. Colon surface voxels whose shape index and curvedness are within a predefined range are selected as initial seeds. Voxels are then clustered by spatial density rules to form lesion candidates. One or more classifiers may then be employed to reduce the false positive rate. Four views of a CAD-detected lesion are shown in Figure 3.6.

As shape features play an important role in this identification of polyp candidates, false positives often showed polyp-like morphology [205]. Similarly, these CAD systems tended to have a higher false negative rate on the same kinds of lesions missed by radiologists, i.e. on the lesions presenting a form factor markedly different from the cap-like shaped, and in particular on flat lesions, which also often have a more subtle appearance [205]. False positives may lead to unnecessary further workups such as polypectomy by colonoscopy; therefore, knowledge about the pattern of CAD false positives is important for dismissing them. Due to the methodology underlying CAD candidate extraction, it is not surprising that many of the false positives detected by CAD tend to exhibit polyp-like shapes [205].

As the intuitive reader may now start to expect, deep learning solutions have been proposed in this domain also, both for electronic cleansing [206] and as a CAD solution [207]. Interestingly though, as labeled data on CT colonography is not as abundant as in other applications such as mammography, the previous CAD systems have been used to create labeled examples on which to train the deep learning CAD.

3.3.3 CAD in Mammography and Digital Breast Tomosynthesis

Full-field digital mammography (FFDM) is today considered the most cost-effective screening method for the early detection of breast cancer. Mammography can reveal both clear evidence of abnormalities, presenting as masses or micro-calcifications clusters, as well as subtle signs such as bilateral asymmetry and architectural distortions, each being characterized by distinctive radiological features [172]. Despite the apparent simplicity of the mammary gland, interpretation of breast imagery requires significant expertise: on the one hand, the masking effect caused by fibroglandular tissue superposition in 2D projection images affects both sensitivity and specificity; on the other hand, screening mammography is often portrayed as the classic "needle in a haystack" kind of problem, due to the low prevalence of cancer in screening populations.

In three-dimensional digital breast tomosynthesis (DBT), multiple projections are acquired over a short angle in order to reconstruct multiple images at different depths, thus effectively limiting tissue superposition while maintaining the dose roughly comparable to that of digital mammography [208]. While DBT improves lesion detection, especially of masses and architectural distortions, the increased cost of equipment, the minor increase in dose and finally its impact on the radiologists' reporting times are slowing down its penetration in mass screening programs.

The potential benefits of breast CAD technology have motivated a very active and long-standing field of research, both in academic and industrial settings. ImageChecker (R2 Technology, Sunnyvale, CA) was the first commercial CAD to be cleared for use by the FDA, followed by several others with ample studies in literature [125,130,152,153,209,210]. Being the subject of extensive research in the past 25 years, an exceptional number of techniques have been proposed in literature, as summarized in by a number of well written surveys and books [170,172,211]. We will here review the main principle in the context of both classical and deep learning approaches.

3.3.3.1 Detection of lesions in mammography and tomosynthesis

Detection of lesions in mammography usually integrates multiple algorithms dedicated to specific radiological signs, and only recently algorithms were proposed that tackle mammography interpretation in a more holistic manner.

Detection of lesions in tomosynthesis is a direct extension of 2D mammography, for which two fundamental approaches exist [212]. In one approach, projections are combined by tomosynthesis reconstruction into a three-dimensional volume, on which dedicated algorithms are run. The image quality of the reconstructed DBT slices, and thus the performance of the CAD system, will depend on the reconstruction algorithm and its parameters, but the conspicuity and visibility of lesions is greatly improved. Another approach is to use the individual projections as input, and then merge information extracted from them. Algorithms developed for regular mammograms can be applied to individual projections, and only an information fusion scheme will be needed to complete the process. Both approaches can be applied alternatively or in combination.

The traditional architecture of CAD for tomosynthesis or mammography is shown in Figure 3.7: each type of lesion (soft tissue lesions and microcalcification clusters) has a dedicated pipeline where initial candidates are detected and then characterized using classification techniques. Microcalcifications are detected on each image, and then grouped in two- or three-dimensional clusters based on their proximity; isolated calcifications are discarded in the process, as they bear no clinical significance.

Broadly speaking, traditional methods to detect and segment initial lesion candidates fall into two main categories: supervised and unsupervised segmentation techniques.

Supervised segmentation, or model-based methods, rely on prior knowledge about the object and background regions to be segmented. Such methods include a training stage to learn the specific objects to be detected; in this specific case, examples of masses and normal mammograms are used to train the system. Based on the training set, the system learns which features are associated with the presence of masses by applying one of many pattern matching techniques, such as neural networks, fuzzy classifiers or statistical inference [211].

Alternatively, unsupervised segmentation partitions an image into a set of regions which are distinct and uniform with respect to specific properties, such as grey-level, texture or colour. Classical approaches to unsupervised segmentation include region-based methods, which divide the image into homogeneous and spatially connected regions; contour-based methods, which rely on the

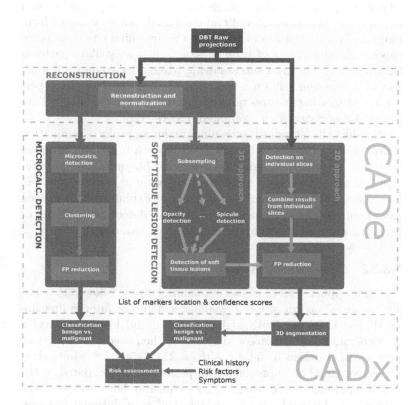

Figure 3.7 Overall architecture of a CAD system for digital breast tomosynthesis. First, reconstruction algorithms are applied to generate the three-dimensional volume from 2D projections. Separate pipelines are applied for the detection of microcalcification clusters (left) and mass candidates (right). Processing can be applied to the reconstructed volume, the individual projections or both as illustrated for the detection of soft tissue lesions; for simplicity, the pipeline for the detection of microcalcification clusters is reported only once. Once detected, lesions can be characterized in terms of their potential of malignancy.

boundaries of regions to be segmented, and clustering methods, which group together those pixels having the same properties and might result in non-connected regions. Features are extracted from biologically inspired filters (such as the Iris filter) that enhance specific characteristics of target lesions, such as stellate patterns [125,172,213]. The most successful approaches based on traditional feature extraction rely on a combination of several feature types, e.g. by integrating features targeting rounded opacities and stellate patterns associated with spiculated masses [125].

Finally, the standard screening mammography examination comprises four projection images - two for each breast - acquired in both craniocaudal (CC) and mediolateral-oblique (MLO) orientations, which are repeated regularly at a yearly or biennial interval. Hence a CAD system must be capable of exploiting information from multiple views or images, and possibly detect asymmetries or temporal changes that may be indicative of pathology.

3.3.3.2 Deep learning in mammography

The first applications of CNNs in mammography followed the classic "cascade" design of CAD systems: a detector filter is first applied that identifies (with high sensitivity and low specificity) a series of candidate regions, and a CNN is then used to classify suspect areas in lesions or false positives [214,215]. The results show a positive trend of improvement in performance compared to the use of hand-engineered features. Some authors have achieved positive results by combining traditional and convolutional features, probably because traditional features allow to provide contextual information complementary to the visual characteristics measured on a localized region of the image [215,216]. The results, however, are limited by the performance of the initial filter, and do not take into account the overall structure of the breast.

A more interesting approach is to tackle detection of abnormalities in the whole breast image. This requires establishment of ground truth at the image or lesion level; the most common approach is to distinguish cases with biopsy-proven cancer from the others, although a few authors have also tackled the task of distinguishing recalled from non-recalled cases. We will return to the issue of establishing ground truth in more detail in Chapter 4.

As illustrated in Figure 3.8, architectures that have been used fall under various categories. Patch-level image analysis, reported in Figure 3.8a, is the simplest implementation and directly verifies

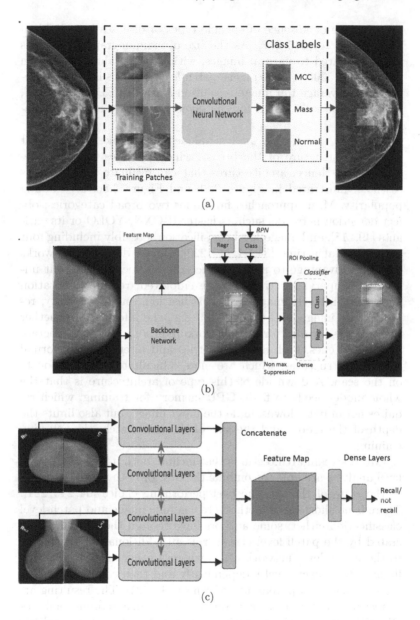

Figure 3.8 Comparison of deep learning architectures for automatic mammography interpretation: from patch-level image analysis (a), to object detection networks such as Faster R-CNN (b), to whole breast image analysis (c).

the presence or absence of specific types of diseases in individual patches [99, 214, 215, 217]. As the size of mammography images is large compared to natural images, with typical values ranging in the order of 5000 to 6000 pixels, patch-level analysis is typically required to leverage full image resolution on both FFDM and DBT, which is especially useful for the detection of tiny microcalcifications.

However, patch-level analysis alone cannot take into account the global structure of the breast, which provides rich interpretative cues. Hence, architectures that can evaluate the breast as a whole, illustrated in Figure 3.8b and Figure 3.8c, are gaining popularity. Most approaches fall under two broad categories: object detection networks such as Faster R-CNN, YOLO or its variants [49, 218], and image-level classification, possibly including four projections at a time [54, 64, 219, 220]. Object detection networks have the advantage to provide precise lesion localization, but unless semi-supervised strategies are employed, require annotation at the lesion level. Image-level classification, on the contrary, requires only image-level supervision (e.g., the information whether the case was recalled for further workup or not), and can integrate also global cues, such as asymmetries and alterations in normal glandular structures, which are more difficult to precisely locate on the scan. A downside of this type of architecture is that the whole model needs to fit in GPU memory for training, which requires not only to downsample the input image, but also limits the depth of the model and the size of the mini-batch, thus slowing training.

Multi-stream architectures that include both image and patch-level analysis are able to combine the best of both worlds and are, at the state of the art, the best performing choice [64, 219, 221]. There is no shortage of methods to combine image and patch-level classification either: some authors have treated the heatmap generated by the patch-level classifier as an additional input channel to the image-level network [219], whereas other authors generate findings from each level independently and then combine them to achieve an overall probability of cancer [64, 221]. The resulting architecture is not necessarily trained end-to-end, and often combines DL with other methods, such as random forests or probabilistic techniques. This approach can be extended to integrate several types of findings or features, including temporal changes with respect to prior images, clinical history and patient demographics [221, 222].

Performance data reported in the literature are dependent on the amount of data available, also taking into account the low prevalence of cancers in mammography screening and the heterogeneity of vendors. An overview of selected papers is presented in Table 3.1.

Large scale datasets ranging from 9,000 to 250,000 patients have been shown to obtain very high performance, close to expert-level. Two recent papers (one in the US [219] and one in Europe [153]) compared the performance of deep learning-based methods with those of experienced radiologists. Wu and colleagues performed a reader study with 14 readers reading 740 exams [219]. Readers were asked to provide a probability estimate of malignancy on a 0%-100% scale for each breast. The deep learning model achieved an Area Under the ROC Curve (AUC) of 0.876, whereas the AUCs achieved by individual readers ranged from 0.705 to 0.860 (mean: 0.778, std: 0.0435). In the second study by Rodriguez-Ruiz and colleagues, nine multi-reader, multi-case study datasets previously used in research studies from seven countries were collected, yielding a total of 2652 exams interpreted by 101 radiologists (28,296 independent interpretations). The AI system achieved a 0.840 AUC, whereas the average performance of the individual radiologist was 0.814 (95% CI = 0.787 to 0.841). The AI system had an AUC higher than 61.4% of the radiologists. While the results of these studies are extremely encouraging, a limitation is that the specific task studied is only part of the diagnostic pipeline, which involves also review of prior exams and clinical history (and in Europe, independent reading by two radiologists), as well as additional diagnostic images acquired in case findings are detected in mammography.

When comparing the size of different training sets, readers are advised to pay attention to the source of training data, as often highly enriched datasets are used given the low cancer prevalence in screening. Transfer learning is commonly used in literature even for large scale datasets, either directly from ImageNet or by bridging through similar modalities, such as older screen-film mammography scans. The heterogeneity of results in literature, even on comparable architectures, underlines the importance of aspects such as network initialization, preprocessing techniques and data augmentation (which often intelligently exploits domain-specific information).

Table 3.1 Overview of selected publications employing deep learning in mammography and tomosynthesis.

Reference	Modality	Task	Method	Training set	Performance
Fotin [214]	DBT	CADe (mass)	Candidate generation through a conventional CAD pipeline followed by CNN (Alexnet-like)	1864 lesions (MG), 339 leisons (DBT)	93% sensitivity at 3.1 mean FP per image
Zhu [223]	MG	CADe (mass)	End-to-end deep multi-instance learning networks	INbreast dataset (115 cases, 80% as training)	AUC = 0.86
Yi [224]	MG	CADx (mass)	Multi-modal CNN combines CC and MLO views	Subset of DDSM (2,085 cases)	AUC = 0.91
Dunghel [216]	MG	mass	Cascade of CNNs for mass detection and classification, pre-training by approximating hand-crafted features	INbreast dataset (115 cases, 80% as training)	AUC = 0.95
Al-masni [218]	MG	CADe (mass)	YOLO architecture is used to extract features, classification is performed by F-CNN	DDSM (2620 cases, 80% as training)	AUC = 0.96
Mordang [225]	MG	CADe (MCC)	Patch-level cascaded CNN: the first CNN eliminates easy false positives, the second CNN performs the final classification	1,000,000 patches (300 patients)	99.92% sensitivity at 0.1 false positive rate
Kooi [215]	MG	CADe (mass)	Patch-level CNN for feature extraction followed by random forest for classification	213,450 patches (6,729 patients)	AUC = 0.941

Samala [99]	MG, DBT	CADx (mass)	ROI-level CNN (AlexNet), dual-transfer learning strategy	1,545 ROIs (MG), 1140 ROIs (DBT)	AUC = 0.82 (DBT), 0.88 (CNN)
Wang [226]	MG	CADe (MCC+mass)	Hand-engineered features are used to train a stacked CNN auto-encoder for feature extraction	1,000 images with lesions	AUC = 0.9
Ribli [49]	MG	CADe (mass)	Faster R-CNN object detection	DDSM + private dataset (2,834 cases)	AUC = 0.95 - 90% sensitivity at 0.3 fp marks
Lotter [220]	MG	CADe (presence/absence of cancer)	Multi-scale CNN (patch-level + image-level) with curriculum learning strategy	DDSM (2,620 cases, 87% training)	AUC = 0.92
Teare [64]	MG	CADe (presence/absence of cancer)	Two CNN architectures to detect lesions at different scales are combined with a random forest gating network	1739 images	AUC = 0.92
Wu [219]	MG	CADe (presence/absence of cancer)	Multi-stream, multi-view CNN architecture for patch-level and image-level classification	229,426 cases	AUC = 0.895

Note: Various tasks are treated differently in the literature. Some authors [64, 219, 220] directly classify images for presence or absence of disease and others perform detection at lesion level. Several figures of merit are reported in the literature. We include only AUC or sensitivity at a given false positive (FP) rate, depending on whether ROC or FROC was used for evaluation. Section 4.2.4.3 defines these terms.

Abbreviations: DBT = digital breast tomosynthesis. MG = manual grading.

Finally, it is worth noticing that applications are not limited to lesion detection; CADx is also an important area of research, which entails predicting outcome in an effort to improve the efficacy of the recall and reduce the number of useless biopsies performed [227]. CADx is usually implemented via patch-level classification, starting from the radiologist input or from the results of a CADe pipeline; however, CBIR-based techniques have also proved useful diagnostic aids.

3.3.4 Diabetic Retinopathy

Diabetic retinopathy (DR) is a progressive disease secondary to diabetes and one of the leading causes of vision loss in the adult population. Visual impairment due to this pathology may occur in at least 10% of subjects affected by diabetes, which in turn affects more than 400 million people worldwide [228, 229]. Early detection and management of the disease can have a great impact in containing the risks and progression of the disease, and may reduce by more than 90% the risk of severe vision loss [228].

Unfortunately, the unavailability of adequate resources and in particular the lack of a sufficient number of clinical experts adversely affects the implementation of screening for this disease, especially in developing countries or in disadvantaged areas. The prevalence of the disease translates into great data availability (a positive factor) and severe clinical impacts (negative) revealed by screening, and coupled with clinician scarcity makes this a great domain for the application of artificial intelligence techniques.

Ocular disease in general has, for a long time, attracted the attention of developers of medical AI. In fact, a review article published in 2014 by Zhang and colleagues on CAD systems applied to ocular diseases cites work ranging back to 1973 [134], when a first contribution describing the segmentation of vessels in retinal images was published (Figure 3.9). With specific reference to DR, previous work was focused on identifying lesions and typically predicting presence or absence of disease, rather than on the assessment of the level of DR. In general, the approach followed classical machine learning methodology: features were extracted and fed into a classifier, which then expressed a binary (or in a few cases 5 level) class for each case. Validation datasets were also of limited size, generally around 100 images.

In 2016, a work by Pratt and colleagues published the results obtained by applying a CNN network to 5-level classification of DR

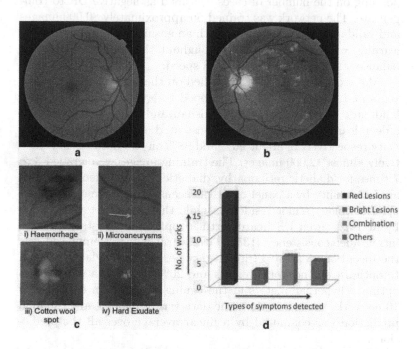

Figure 3.9 Diabetic retinopathy (DR) lesions in deep fundus photographs (DFPs) of retina: DFP of normal eye (a), eye affected by DR (b), four types of DR lesions (c) and descriptions of lesions in review by Zhang et al. [134]. Figure adapted with permission from Zhang et al. "A survey on computer aided diagnosis for ocular diseases." *BMC Medical Informatics and Decision Making*, 14(1):80, 2014.

pathology [136]. As in similar applications we cite in this book, the main difficulties encountered were related to the strong imbalance in case level in the database, with few presentations of level 4 and 5 cases and a majority of normal cases. For every batch loaded for back-propagation, class weights were updated with a ratio depending on the number of cases classified as negative DR to compensate. The network was trained on approximately 80,000 images and validated on 5,000 images, with an ensuing 75% accuracy. The learning rate was modulated throughout the training process to balance stability, effectiveness and speed.

Many other works were published on the topic in the following years and indeed are being developed today. Again in 2016, in a landmark paper published by Gulshan and colleagues in *JAMA*, a deep learning architecture demonstrated a sensitivity and specificity respectively of about 90% and 98% on two datasets of collectively almost 12,000 images. The training images were graded 3 to 7 times for diabetic retinopathy, diabetic macular edema, and image gradability by a panel of 54 US licensed ophthalmologists and ophthalmology senior residents, while the testing set was graded by at least seven US board-certified ophthalmologists with high intragrader consistency [135]. The neural network employed was the Inception-v3 architecture. Eighty percent of the data was used to optimize the network weights and 20% of the data was used to optimize hyperparameters in the tuning process. An ensemble of 10 networks trained on the same data was developed, and the final prediction was computed by a linear average over all the predictions.

These impressive performances were further confirmed in a subsequent work [230]. In this prospective observational study conducted in two eye centers in India, 3,049 patients with diabetes were examined for DR or referable diabetic macula edema. The AI system's results were compared with manual grading by one trained grader and one retina specialist from each site. In case of disagreement, adjudication by a panel of 3 retinal specialists served as the reference standard.

For moderate or worse DR, the sensitivity and specificity for individual graders (not including the readers who performed adjudication) ranged from 73.4% to 89.8% and from 83.5% to 98.7%, respectively. The AI system's performance yielded an 88.9% sensitivity (95% CI, 85.8-91.5), and a 92.2% specificity (95% CI, 90.3-93.8) on the data set from the first center and a 92.1% sensitivity (95% CI, 90.1-93.8), with 95.2% specificity (95% CI, 94.2-96.1) on the data set from the second center, thus exhibiting a performance equal to or exceeding that of the individual graders.

Considering the limited time frame from 2016 to now, the research on this topic has continued to progress with surprising breadth and depth. In a work by Poplin and colleagues published in 2018 in *Nature Biomedical Engineering* [231], authors were able to predict with a deep learning network cardiovascular risk factors such as age, gender, systolic blood pressure and risk of cardiovascular adverse events from retinal fundus photographs, information which was previously not known to be present in the images. In another work exploring a completely different aspect, AI automatic detection of DR pathology was applied to smartphone fundus photographs, exhibiting a high level of sensitivity [232], and thus offering promise for a further facilitated pathway to diagnosis and care. In the meanwhile, improvements on the technology through the construction of ever more accurate reference standards are being explored [233]. These are interesting times for this field and we are very curious about future developments.

CHAPTER 4

Designing AI Systems for Clinical Practice

Designing an artificial intelligence system presenting excellent performances, maybe even on par with human experts, may appear as a daunting task, and indeed requires significant efforts. When however the development goes beyond the preliminary research phase and the system starts to exhibit promise, the challenge of appropriately validating the system in order to ensure a safe and effective use in clinical practice emerges. Indeed, as we will see in the following, in many cases it is advisable to outline the validation process even before the actual development of the system itself. In our experience, the clinical validation, along with the data collection phase, are the longest and most costly steps in the development of artificial intelligence systems for medical practice.

In the initial years, software systems were mostly embedded in hardware medical devices, and thus the primary concern was guarding against the possibility of physical harm, with attention to aspects such as the transmission of energy and/or substances to or from the body, the degree of invasiveness, the closeness to sensitive organs, etc. This was reflected in many of the regulatory directives and guidelines, which often did not offer specific indications for software developed as a standalone clinical aid. As the use of such applications steadily grew, the need for specific guidance was felt and several contributions were developed, which we will here try to describe.

This chapter is organized as follows. In the first section, we will introduce the concept of medical devices constituted by standalone software. In the second section, we will describe relevant concepts for the validation of AI/ML applications in the medical field. Many of these notions were originally introduced in articles and guidelines for computer aided detection and diagnosis software, but represent in our view a general overview of many of the issues to consider when designing and testing AI software for medical use. We also present emerging approaches to the validation of AI/ML software devices that evolve continuously in time, and thus are challenging for most current regulatory frameworks where changes to a device require regulatory approval prior to public use.

Finally, the application of AI/ML systems in clinical practice has been postulated as a mechanism by which better health outcomes and/or lower costs of the care could be achieved. In the last section of chapter, we will address the important topic of how to define the ultimate clinical utility of a device, and describe how randomized trials and other study designs can be used to evaluate it.

4.1 SOFTWARE AS A MEDICAL DEVICE

In 2014 a draft document (finalized in 2017) issued by the International Medical Device Regulators Forum (IMDRF) introduced the following definition of Software as a Medical Device (SaMD): "Software intended to be used for one or more medical purposes that perform these purposes without being part of a hardware medical device" [234]. In the same document, specific risks of this kind of device are also described, such as the possible dependence of performance on the deployment on different hardware platforms, or the management of updates, which may be performed by inexperienced users, or the risks related to the duplication of software outside of the control of the manufacturer. In the IMDRF report, the working group proposes a framework to assess the risk that a SaMD may pose. This kind of evaluation is very important, as it may guide the clinical validation pathway for public use approval.

Risk management principles play an important role in many disciplines, as they provide a framework for minimizing the probability of adverse outcomes, which in the medical device industry typically translates into harm for users, whether patients or

Table 4.1 Levels of risk associated with SaMD evaluation.

State of healthcare situation or condition	Significance of information provided by SaMD to healthcare decision		
	Treat or diagnose	Drive clinical management	Inform clinical management
Critical	IV	III	II
Serious	III	II	I
Non-serious	II	I	I

Source: Software as a Medical Device Working Group. Software as a medical device (SaMD): Clinical evaluation. http://www.imdrf.org/docs/imdrf/final/technical/imdrf-tech-170921-samd-n41-clinical-evaluation-1.pdg. Accessed 2019-07-28.

healthcare providers. In the cited framework, two dimensions are specified as describing the level of risk posed by a SaMD to a subject. The first is the *significance of the information* provided by the SaMD to the healthcare decision, which may be classified as informing the clinical management, driving the clinical management or diagnosing and/or treating. The second is the *state of the healthcare situation or condition*, which may be non-serious, serious or critical. When combined, the two dimensions determine the level of risk carried by the medical device, which may vary from level I, low impact, in case of a non-serious or serious conditions in which the SaMD simply informs clinical management to level IV risk, very high impact, which arises when the SaMD has the objective of treating or diagnosing a patient in case of a clinically critical situation. The possible combinations and the corresponding level of impact are shown in Table 4.1.

Considerations which help in categorizing the significance are whether the software triggers an immediate or near term action or simply provides additional information, while the criticality of the clinical situation depends on factors such as the seriousness of the medical condition, the time criticality of the information provided in relation to the development of the pathological condition and the fragility of the patients (e.g. use in a pediatric population). The interested reader is referred to the final 2017 report by IMDRF [234], where these topics are described in depth and several examples are provided to further clarify these important issues.

4.2 CLINICAL EVALUATION OF SaMD

Up to the first decade of year 2000, even though many computer aided detection/diagnosis applications had been developed, both for commercial use and in academia, the comparison of the different systems proved difficult (and to a certain extent, this problem still remains). The problem was rooted in the lack of a standardized approach to evaluating and reporting CAD performances. In general, the need for structured guidelines for assessing CAD performance and for performing quality assurance in clinical practice was felt. This led to the constitution of a working group by American Association of Physicists in Medicine, the Computer Aided Detection in Diagnostic Imaging Subcommittee (CADSC), who issued two contributions with the objective of drawing attention to these problems and to provide a starting point for future recommendations on best practices for CAD validation [175, 235].

The FDA guidance for CAD issued in 2012, "Computer-Assisted Detection Devices Applied to Radiology Images and Radiology Device Data - Premarket Notification [510(k)] Submissions" further developed these concepts and established recommendations for the regulatory approval of CAD devices. In these contributions, many cardinal aspects of clinical validation still valid for AI systems today are discussed, such as the potential sources of bias in training and testing, the construction of the reference standard for evaluation and metrics for the evaluation of performance.

As AI applications to the clinical field continue to increase and diversify, more comprehensive frameworks have been recently proposed, which embrace a larger scope and are addressed to all SaMD. This approach, again developed by the IMDRF working group [234], is more general, in that it describes all the steps that are necessary to assure the quality of SaMD.

This framework introduces a preliminary phase in which a valid association between the SaMD output and the clinical condition which the device is targeting has to be demonstrated. New applications are constantly being designed, coupling information together in novel ways and generating innovative outputs, potentially leading to real clinical benefits. This step may be performed by completing searches in literature, through original clinical research or by consulting professional society guidelines if such evidence is already existing, otherwise it may require the generation of new evidence through clinical trials or by secondary analyses on existing data.

The next phase explicitly considered in the IMDRF document, therein defined as analytical validation, is the demonstration of verification and validation activities characteristic of good engineering practices and quality management systems. Specifically this phase should provide evidence that the software "correctly and reliably processes input data and generates output data with the appropriate level of accuracy, and repeatability and reproducibility", meets specifications, which must conform to user needs and to intended uses [234].

Finally, the last phase foreseen is the clinical validation, which we will cover more extensively in the following section.

4.2.1 Clinical Validation of SaMD

When considering the clinical validation of a medical system (and indeed when designing the system as a whole), one of the first elements which must be taken into account is how the system will be integrated in the clinical workflow.

In some cases, SaMDs are used as measuring devices, for instance to estimate lesion size or diameter, and it is sufficient to validate the accuracy of such measurements. Less likely at the state of the art, they may deliver a final diagnosis or indication of treatment, as in the case of triage systems. In most cases, however, software offers indications to a clinician or healthcare operator, and hence the clinical evaluation must take into account the performance of the clinician when using the software.

Clinical validation is thus generally divided in two phases, i.e. a first phase in which the system performance is evaluated standalone, and a second phase, which usually entails a clinical study, in which the impact of the system is evaluated within the workflow itself. This can be done either in a prospective way, which completely mimics the normal processing of cases, or in a laboratory study on retrospective data. This second phase is very important, because it yields the best measure of how effective the system will be in true clinical practice; it may be avoided when a comparable system is already available, and clinical equivalence can be established through direct comparison.

As an example, an AI system indicating suspect lesions which has demonstrated perfect sensitivity in identifying lesions in a standalone validation may not be able to guarantee that all true lesions are included in the final report, because the clinician may decide not to confirm the suggested lesions. A real-life example is shown in

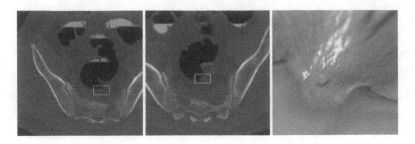

Figure 4.1 The axial CT scan shows an 8 mm polyp of the sigmoid colon on the prone scan (a), supine scan (b) and endoluinal view (c) in CT colonography. The lesion was prompted by the CAD system, but was subsequently rejected by the radiologist reviewing the case. Image reproduced from Morra et al., "Computer-Aided Diagnosis for X-ray Imaging" in *Handbook of X-ray Imaging: Physics and Technology* [204].

Figure 4.1. There are many reasons for which this may be the case: for example, the false positive rate of the system may be too high, so that the clinician has difficulty distinguishing the true prompts from the false suggestions or even worse loses trust in the system and disregards the suggestions altogether. In CT colonography, for instance, the theoretical capacity of identifying lesions of the radiologist plus the system, defined as the sum of the lesions seen by the radiologist and those prompted by the system, was almost always higher than that observed when the radiologist employed the system in a clinical context. In other cases, the user interface may be confusing or the output of the system unclear. Examples of CAD-radiologist interaction paradigms, which we omit here for brevity, may be found in [204].

Notwithstanding these limitations, a standalone evaluation of the performances of the system is an important step, because it reveals the magnitude of the potential impact (or inherent limitations) of the system, prior to testing of the performance with the clinician in the loop. Another advantage is that it provides a measure of the system performance independent of the human factor, which introduces inter- and intra-operator variabilities that complicate evaluation.

Clinical studies may vary in design, depending in first place on the kind of interaction between clinician and system, but both clinical and standalone studies require that the proper attention is paid in the process of collection and use of the data, and they often share evaluation metrics. These are the aspects that we will describe in the following subsections. These elements were originally identified specifically for CAD devices [175], but many of these considerations, if not all, may find a general applicability in other AI systems. The reader should bear in mind that the elements here introduced are a non-exhaustive introduction to the evaluations which may be carried out. Furthermore, a continuous exploration of additional considerations related to new kinds of use cases will probably be necessary in the future, as the applications for medical AI spread and diversify.

4.2.2 Data Collection: Factors Affecting Performance

Many factors inherently present in the data may influence the outcome of a performance assessment and it is extremely difficult, if not impossible, to avoid all sources of bias. A depiction of the main sources of variability is shown in Figure 4.2. All the variables pertaining to the distribution of the disease on the subjects may be relevant: age, sex, race, presence of risk factors or symptoms may influence among other factors the prevalence and form of the disease.

In general, when the sample dataset population is not representative of the population on which the AI system will be applied, *spectrum* or *selection bias* may occur. Thus, the population on which the device is to be applied must be specified in the intended use and new evaluations may be necessary when use is extended to new populations. This is particularly true when intended use expands to include fragile subgroups, e.g. pediatric subjects, but may be also very important when apparently the new use case is less critical, e.g. when extending use from a symptomatic to a screening population, as in the second case the lesions are often smaller and less evident. An indirect effect of the population may also emerge: for example, in screening it is particularly important to reduce dose, as much as possible, which as we will see below impacts image quality. The clinical pathway may also be important for other considerations, as the target for the system may vary depending on the application.

Another aspect which may strongly influence results is patient preparation for the exam. In CT colonography, for example, the administration of different contrast agents can change rather drastically the appearance of the tagged residue in the images, with an impact on the performance of CAD systems designed to detect lesions [236, 237].

In the specific context of SaMDs operating on medical images, all the parameters related to the image acquisition and processing are also very relevant and must be clearly specified. Most imaging scanners are not calibrated measurement devices, and allow for wide variations in acquisition, reconstruction and post-processing protocols, often through proprietary image processing techniques that were primarily designed to be interpretable by humans, rather than computers [32]. Imaging equipment and acquisition protocol (including aspects such as image resolution, acquisition angles, number of images, etc.) may have a very strong impact on the image quality and detectability of the disease. In X-ray images, dose has a strong influence on image quality and specifically contrast-to-noise-ratio. In response to concerns about the risk of radiation-induced cancer, especially in healthy subjects or in the case of frequently repeated tests, imaging protocols and reconstruction techniques have been introduced to reduce dose while preserving image quality, however the effect on image readability may be very different in humans and computerized systems [238, 239].

This consideration is true in general: more often than not, AI systems are much more sensitive than humans to subtle variations in image intensity distributions, because they rely on quantitative features directly or indirectly extracted from the images. In the future, as the corpus of data available grows and training algorithms become more robust to domain shifts, as discussed in Chapter 2, this may no longer be the case, but until now specific testing is certainly warranted. As a consequence, differences in the image post-processing chain may also strongly impact system performance. Image reconstruction in the case of volumetric scans, or post-processing for image enhancement or to provide an *ad-hoc* look-and-feel requested by the clinician, may alter images and the results of the applied AI systems.

In general, the supported range of equipment, acquisition and reconstruction parameters, and other relevant factors should be specified in the validation procedure and users need to be aware that substantial deviation from these parameters may affect system performance. This is especially true in those cases in which disease progression is monitored in time, as it is important to ensure that observed changes are truly reflective of anatomical or functional modifications, and not of differences in the equipment or acquisition protocol [235, 240].

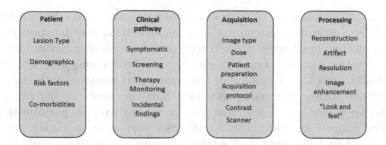

Figure 4.2 Factors affecting AI system performance. Different kinds of factors which may have an impact on the evaluation of performance are shown, e.g. through a modification of disease detectability or by selection bias.

4.2.3 Training and Testing Datasets

One of the most important steps in the machine learning process is the definition of the datasets employed for the training and the testing of the system.

A first fundamental observation is that in order to assess a system's performance, the set of data used for testing must be independent from the data used for training. In fact, the use of the training data to compute system performance usually leads to an optimistically biased measure of performance, as the system may overfit the data, learning non-general features specifically related to the examples. A repeated use of the testing set to evaluate performance is also non optimal, as it may lead to an implicit choice of parameters which are more performant on the testing set. For this reason, intermediate test sets named validation sets are employed and ideally the testing set should be sequestered from the researchers developing the system and its use tracked.

Another important point in building training and testing sets is the composition of the sample. We have already seen in the previous section the factors which may influence a system's performance and which must be taken into consideration when composing the training and testing sets. In principle, a training set should contain enough data to estimate the parameters of the system, should present sufficiently varied examples of positive and negative cases, should be representative of the population (although in some cases over-representing some types, e.g. the more difficult lesions, may present advantages). In practice, this may not always be possible, so numerous strategies of data augmentation may be applied, as outlined in Chapter 2.2.2. If representativeness is important for the training set, it is even more fundamental for testing sets, which should allow the evaluation of the system performance on the target population. In some applications, however, most notably when disease prevalence is low, test set enrichening may be performed. The manner by which the set is enrichened must be clearly explained and inclusion and exclusion criteria must be stated. In general, a thorough description of all the relevant variables of the training and testing data may be very important to fully understand system performance and must be included in the documentation regarding the validation.

4.2.4 Performance Assessment of CAD Devices

4.2.4.1 Reference standard

In most cases, the objective of medical AI systems, and especially CAD devices, is the identification or characterization of pathology. Hence, a number of cases in which the disease state (presence, absence, extent, etc.) is known are necessary to establish performance. In many cases, however, a perfect knowledge of the state of the disease may not be possible. Even employing only cases in which the disease state is absolutely certain is not a solution, as often these cases have peculiar characteristics (typically the disease is at an advanced stage) and therefore what is called *verification bias* may occur.

When a definite assessment of the state of the disease is possible, typically through an independent modality, the reference standard may be named "ground truth" or "gold standard". Even in this case however the reference standard may be imperfect, as no methodology presents an absolutely zero error rate. Optical colonoscopy is considered the reference standard for CT colonography, yet a review of tandem colonoscopy studies by van Rijn and colleagues reported pooled miss rates for polyps of 22% [241]. Even biopsies are known to carry a certain error rate.

When the reference standard is obtained through an independent modality and the task requires the localization of the disease the issue of correctly matching the lesions found on the images with those of the control modality may arise. In these cases, the criteria employed for matching the lesions must be defined.

There are cases in which there are no independent means of ascertaining the state of disease of a case, as may be possible in some cases in lung radiological exams, in which biopsy is not possible or not warranted. In these cases, typically a panel of experts evaluates the cases and establishes a reference standard. One such example is the Lung Image Database Consortium and Image Database Resource Initiative (LIDC/IDRI), in which a reference standard on more than one thousand cases was built employing the evaluations of four expert radiologists per case [128].

The reference standard should be constructed considering the intended use of the AI system. In some cases, simply ascertaining the presence or absence of the disease may be enough, in others there may be additional information which must be collected, such as the extent and localization of the disease. When additional information must be predicted by the system, this information must be present in the reference standard as well. In any case, a clear specification of the target is important (e.g. are the statistics provided at lesion level or at patient level?), as performances may vary significantly.

4.2.4.2 Mark-labeling criteria

When testing AI systems with the intended use of detecting target lesions, criteria for determining whether or not the prompt proposed by the software is actually signaling the lesion in the reference standard must be defined. This process is named mark-labeling. When the prompt is superimposed to the lesion to detect this may seem fairly obvious, but it many cases the overlap between prompt and target may only be partial. This occurs more frequently in cases, such as mammography, where the search space is limited and the probability of having a chance superimposition is higher.

Criteria proposed in literature include simple overlap between target and prompt, thresholds on area (or volume) of intersection over union or distance between the centroids. A de-facto standard may be established for some applications, but in many cases a variety of different methods are commonly used. Different matching criteria may lead to different results in validation, thus it is always important to specify matching criteria. A visual exam may reveal shortcomings in the criteria applied and may be admitted in some cases for correction. Importantly, however, the criteria for matching must always be defined before performing testing.

4.2.4.3 Performance metrics: Sensitivity, specificity and ROC analysis

Once the reference standard has been established and the mark-labeling criteria have been identified, the capacity of the system of determining presence or absence of disease may be evaluated. Cases correctly identified as presenting disease by the system are defined true positives, while cases correctly discarded as negative are true negatives. Conversely, positive cases incorrectly discarded as negative are defined false negatives, and negative cases incorrectly prompted as positives are false positives. Thus, the performance of the system is defined by the so-called confusion matrix depicted in Figure 4.3. The sensitivity of a system may then be defined as the fraction of positive cases identified by the system. This measure quantifies the capability of the system of correctly identifying disease.

Analogously, the specificity is the fraction of negative cases correctly identified and quantifies the capability of the system of discarding negative cases. Often an alternative measure may be employed, which is the false positive rate, equal to 1 - the specificity. If the viewpoint is reversed and one wishes to quantify the probability of disease given the system results, two other descriptors, again deriving from the confusion matrix, may be employed, i.e. the positive predictive value and the negative predictive value. The first term corresponds to the probability of presenting disease given a positive system result, while the second quantifies the probability of absence of disease given negative system result.

This formulation implicitly requires the system to provide a dichotomous result, while in most cases AI systems output continuous values, to which a threshold is be applied to define a case as positive or negative. Given the threshold, technically defined as the operating point, the system will present a specific value of sensitivity and specificity. Thus, the performance of the AI system is completely described when all the sensitivity and specificity couples corresponding to all the possible threshold values are evaluated. If the sensitivity of the system is depicted on the y-axis and the specificity on the x-axis, the curve determined by all possible pairs of specificity-sensitivity values exhibited by the system is the so-called ROC (receiver operating characteristic) curve, which completely defines the potential capabilities of the designed system at all operating points. The ROC curve increases monotonically (Figure 4.4). Lower thresholds classify more cases as positive, and thus generally increase both sensitivity and false positive rate (an

Actual Condition (True/False)
as determined by reference standard

		True	False
Positive		True Positive (TP)	False Positive (FP)
Negative		False Negative (FN)	True Negative (TN)

Predicted outcome (Positive/Negative)

$$\text{Sensitivity} = \frac{TP}{TP + FN} \qquad \text{Specificity} = \frac{TN}{TN + FP}$$

$$\text{PPV} = \frac{TP}{TP + FP} \qquad \text{NPV} = \frac{TN}{TN + FN}$$

Figure 4.3 The confusion matrix summarizes the performance of a classifier for binary classification tasks, comparing the predicted value with a reference standard.

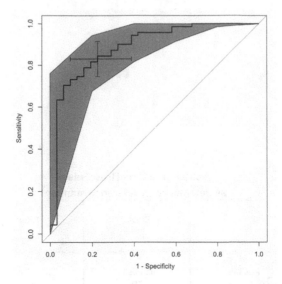

Figure 4.4 Receiver operating characteristics (ROC) curve with confidence interval. The straight line represents the performance of a random classifier.

inverse of the result may be considered if the reverse were true). Higher thresholds limit the false positives, but may increase the number of false negatives as well. In practice, as the number of cases is limited, the modification of the threshold value will not always lead to an experimental increase in the value of the sensitivity or specificity. The experimental ROC curve will thus not be smooth and present a series of steps. To overcome this limitation, parametric ROC curves may be determined by fitting the experimental data, typically assuming an underlying binomial distribution.

Once the curve is determined, different figures of merit which express the global discrimination capabilities of the system may be calculated. A commonly employed figure of merit is the so-called ROC AUC (area under the curve). A perfect classifier correctly classifies all positive cases as positive and all negative cases as negative, and thus presents an AUC equal to 1. The worst possible classifier is not the classifier with AUC equal to 0 that mistakes all the positive cases as negative and vice versa, as in this case it would suffice to invert the classifier decision to have a perfect result. The worst possible result is the random classifier that presents an AUC of 0.5.

Variants of the ROC which take into account the capability of correctly identifying and localizing disease in a case have been defined in literature. In the LROC (localization ROC) paradigm the area which is most likely to present disease is rated for each case, and the fraction of cases which indeed presents a lesion in this area yields the sensitivity of the system. In this paradigm, each image contains at most one lesion, and the observer scores and marks the most suspicious location. In the more general FROC (free-response ROC) paradigm, more than one lesion may be present in the case and the sensitivity is given by the fraction of correctly localized and identified disease cases, while the specificity is expressed through the number of false positives per case. [242].

ROC and FROC analysis may be employed both in standalone assessments and in clinical studies, if clinicians express their evaluation of a case through a non-dichotomous measure, such as their degree of confidence on the presence or absence of disease in a case [243].

Performance evaluation should be based on a sound statistical plan, for instance including confidence intervals for reported figures of merit, testing for statistical significance of differences when comparing multiple systems, and planning for appropriate sample size in clinical studies. The interested reader may refer to [175] for a more ample discussion of the subject.

4.2.5 Clinical Validation of Imaging Biomarkers and Radiomics

Quantitative image analysis (QIA) and radiomics both involve the extraction of quantitative information and features from medical images, as discussed in Chapters 3.2.1 and 3.2.5. Clinical validation shares many common points with CAD and other AI/ML applications. However, while CAD evaluation places emphasis on assessing performance in clinical settings, in QIA validation is shifted towards the intrinsic reproducibility of quantitative measurements across devices, patients and, for repeated measurements, time. This consideration, however, by no means diminishes the importance of accounting for variability across devices and patient populations also in CAD.

A framework for evaluation of quantitative imaging biomarkers (QIB) was proposed by the QIBA Technical Performance Working Group in the paper by Raunig and colleagues [244], but the main principles are also applicable to radiomics [185]. First, it identifies three sources of variations which are the patient, the image acquisition system, and the measurement algorithm; the latter is especially critical in the case of semi-automatic algorithms which entail a manual or semi-manual segmentation. Secondly, several measurements of variability (or better, classes of) are identified, which include *bias* (the difference between the expected value of the biomarker and the measurand, i.e. the true value of the quantity intended to be measured), *linearity* (is a change in the measurand reflected as a proportional change in the biomarker?), *repeatability* (the ability to repeatedly measure the same feature under identical or near-identical conditions, e.g. on the same subject acquired multiple times) and *reproducibility* (the ability to measure the same feature under different conditions expected in clinical practice, e.g. different equipment, software or operators). For instance, if the biomarker is a volumetric measurement, comparison with true volume (when known) or with an acceptable surrogate (e.g. manual segmentation) can be used to ascertain the presence of bias, i.e. systematic errors. Validated phantoms can provide an acceptable reference when the true measure may be unattainable on clinical images. For each of these measurements, several statistical techniques have been proposed in literature [244].

An important aspect of designing a statistical plan for QIB studies is the choice of random or fixed effects, each representing a relevant factor for variability, as well as of stratification factors, if any. For instance, repeatability studies involving patients or subjects will often consider the subjects or patients as a random factor, which allows us to generalize the findings to other patients. On the contrary, acquisition factors with few possible levels or options are often defined as fixed effects, assuming that further departures are unlikely.

Repeatability and reproducibility are also important characteristics of radiomic features, especially when studying their association with prognosis or gene expression, or when cutoffs on specific feature values are defined [185,245]. Selecting features with proven high repeatability and high reproducibility could in turn improve the quality and reproducibility of predictive models. The feature itself may be calculated or defined in slightly different ways in each software implementation, not all of which are publicly available for comparison and inspection. This is especially relevant for deep learning-based features, which depend on the specific model and training and do not lend themselves to a precise mathematical formulation. The reproducibility of deep learning-based features has been less investigated; however, they may be less sensitive to changes in image appearance and quality, as they have been designed and pretrained on natural images that exhibit a large variability in illumination and contrast [32].

The scientific community is still working towards a consensus on how to assess the repeability and/or reproducibility of radiomics. Studies in literature vary in study setup, metrics (among others, intraclass correlation coefficient, concordance correlation coefficient, Spearman correlation) and cutoff values used to segregate stable from unstable features [185]. Certain types of features, e.g. shape and texture, are also strongly affected by variations in the region-of-interest segmentation. This may introduce confounding factors when assessing or comparing certain features or software implementations.

When assessing tumors, regions of interest (ROIs) may be further drawn on subregions such as contrast-enhancing regions, necrosis, and non-enhancing regions. This method results in clustering of observations within each patient, in addition to the clustering due to inter-feature correlation. Radiomics features are often derived from the same base matrices, and hence have strong interclass correlation and are likely to be clustered [245]; they may be also correlated to the volume of the tumor or structure being studied [185]. Clustered data violates the independence assumptions that is the basis for most statistical tests used in literature, leading to misleadingly small estimated standard error. This is an important area of attention for which best practices are still being defined [245].

It is worth noticing that greater reproducibility in the clinical setting can also be achieved through higher standardization of the input images, and hence of the acquisition and processing protocols. More generally speaking, enhancing the reproducibility of the acquisition technique would result in a tangible clinical benefit [246]. Several initiatives are seeking to industrialize quantitative imaging by bringing together the entire spectrum of groups involved in its development and implementation, including vendors of imaging equipment. To this aim, the Radiological Society of North America (RSNA) and the National Institute for Biomedical Imaging and Bioengineering have sponsored the Quantitative Imaging Biomarkers Alliance (QIBA) [247]; among other undertakings, QIBA has proposed standardized profiles for well known biomarkers, such as CT volume changes in CT scans. In Europe, the European Imaging Biomarkers Alliance - EIBALL brings together the key players involved in biomarkers research and application, and promotes the clinical use of biomarkers by setting standards for data acquisition and image processing.

4.3 REGULATORY APPROACHES FOR ADAPTIVE AI DEVICES

As we have seen throughout the book, machine learning systems and many AI applications in general are characterized by their ability to continuously improve as new data accumulates, as is typically the case when a device hits the market. This ease of change differentiates these devices from conventional medical devices and indeed also from many SaMDs, introducing yet again a new issue in regulatory management. As a matter of fact, existing regulatory approaches may require that devices perform a regulatory re-assessment prior to market access in the case of changes to the devices, especially when these changes are substantial. This position is perfectly reasonable, as it helps guarantee the safety and effectiveness of the modified devices, but it is ill suited to the pace of change of ML/AI software. With the current framework, the timing and expense of the regulatory pathway may seriously inhibit the rapid adoption of improved devices, to the detriment of both patients and the industry.

The FDA has recently addressed this challenge and is working on a regulatory framework specifically addressed at continuously learning software devices. At the moment of writing, final guidelines have not yet been issued, but many interesting concepts already emerge in the discussion paper published by FDA in April 2019. In this work, a Total Product Lifecycle Regulatory approach is described in which the assurance of safety and effectiveness of a modified marketed device rests on the demonstration of the organizational excellence, good machine learning practices, quality post-market surveillance, as well as on a predetermined plan for the expected adjustments, defined as the "predetermined change control plan" [248].

This change control plan should describe in particular two aspects: 1) the expected modifications on the device and 2) the methodology by which the manufacturer would introduce the above changes in order to control potential risks to patients and users. These aspects would be covered respectively in the so-called SaMD pre-specifications (SPS) and the algorithm change protocol (ACP).

In the SPS the scope of the modifications are described. Three types of modifications are defined. System performance may be improved through retraining with new data or architectural modifications. Inputs to the system may change, either through an expansion of compatible inputs (e.g. images from new image acquisition equipment) or by inclusion of radically new input data types. Finally, and more importantly, the intended use of the system may change, either through a change in the significance of the information provided (e.g. from informing clinical management to driving clinical management), a wider patient population or through a modification of the intended disease or condition for which the system was designed.

In the ACP, conversely, all the steps of the data and procedures to be followed in order to guarantee that the modified devices remain safe and effective must be described. This detailed description must include many elements: data collection procedures including the management and quality assurance of testing and training datasets; retraining objectives with the description of foreseen changes to preprocessing, ML architecture and methodology; evaluation criteria including metrics and statistical analysis plans, performance targets, triggers for initiating evaluation, clinical validations; and finally update procedures, with software verification, validation and update plans.

In this kind of scenario, it is envisioned that even relatively important changes might be possible without opening a new regulatory procedure. As examples, both an extension of patient population and a modification of the intended use with an increase in the significance of the information provided (e.g. a shift within driving clinical management from identifying early signs of a disease or condition to aid in making a definitive diagnosis). It is however also acknowledged that not all modifications will be feasible, in particular those that entail a significant change in the level of associated risk.

The future is open, many modifications may still take place and different approaches may be followed elsewhere. The discussions and the attention to these new issues however are very encouraging for those in the field. We will be actively following the debate and hopefully so will the reader.

4.4 ESTABLISHING CLINICAL UTILITY FOR AI APPLICATIONS

Despite the impressive results generated in a laboratory setting, where, for instance, deep learning algorithms have been shown to outperform radiologists in specific recognition tasks, so far clinical practice remains largely untouched by this technology [155, 249].

Nearly all of the recent studies on the performance of ML/AI systems for diagnostic analysis of medical images were designed as proof-of-concept (pilot and/or feasibility) studies and lacked the design features recommended for understanding the benefits, harms and costs (direct and indirect) of adoption of ML/AI systems across care settings [155, 249].

An important obstacle to a fast clinical integration of ML/AI systems for diagnosis and/or prediction purposes will be the need to provide robust evidence of clinical utility for ML/AI systems. Clinical utility is related to the ability of a diagnostic test to significantly improve health outcomes in a defined patient population. Broadly speaking, it defines whether the results of an intervention are effective and whether its implementation offers an economically efficient solution to a health care problem, compared with the current standard of care. Clearly, both assessments provide information that is central to making health care decisions.

4.4.1 Clinical Utility: Definition

Initial approval of a medical device for marketing and use in patients, such as premarket clearance through the 510(k) or Premarket Approval Application under regulation by the US Food and Drug Administration (FDA), does not necessarily mean that it improves patient outcomes or should be used. FDA review generally assures a new medical device has established analytical and clinical validity, the latter being defined as the association between the device and the medical condition of interest. The agency does not generally require outcome studies, and so clinical utility of an assay may not be demonstrated at the time of approval or clearance of a diagnostic test.

For example, deep learning systems for analyzing cardiac magnetic resonance images [250] and breast ultrasonographic images [251] have recently received FDA approval or clearance for clinical use. However, clinical adoption of diagnostic or predictive ML/AI models at higher levels, such as acceptance as recommended practice by experts, academic societies, or independent third-party organizations such as the US Preventive Services Task Force, and approval for reimbursement typically require more than measures of a test's analytical or technical performance and diagnostic accuracy. Sufficient evidence that testing improves health outcomes in defined patient populations, enhances healthcare quality and efficiency or reduces costs or resource utilization should be required. Therefore, the final clinical verification of a diagnostic or predictive artificial intelligence tool requires a demonstration of its usefulness on patient management, beyond performance metrics, and subsequent regulatory decisions about its adoption should be made based on proof of clinically important improvements in relevant patient outcomes [252].

Clinical utility in its narrowest sense refers to the ability of a diagnostic test to prevent or ameliorate adverse health outcomes such as mortality, morbidity, or cancer incidence through the adoption of efficacious treatments conditioned on test results. In its broadest sense, clinical utility can refer to any outcomes considered important to patient management. It can take the form of improved efficiency in clinical decision making, streamlined clinical workflow, better patient outcomes, and/or cost offsets or avoidance. Therefore, it is possible that a diagnostic test has clinical utility without actually improving the clinical outcomes of interest. If the introduction of a ML/AI system leads to health outcomes comparable to those obtained with current standard strategies but these outcomes are achieved in a simpler and cheaper way, there may be clinical utility. For example, cancer screening examinations of the breast generate large volumes of imaging data that radiologists must examine. AI approaches that can screen such images automatically would save radiologists' time, staff costs and resources used in the reading process, giving a strong incentive for adoption, particularly in resource-limited screening settings or in large-scale population screening programs that currently rely on double-reading (i.e., independent reviews of breast images by two specially trained radiologists) [152, 176, 204, 253].

As shown in the above example, utility of a diagnostic testing strategy cannot be defined in an absolute sense; it has to be evaluated relative to the current standard of care. In thinking about the utility of a AI system, we do not just evaluate whether using the test intrinsically leads to the outcomes desired; we also compare the outcomes of using the test with the outcomes of using the current best alternative, in similar patients.

The analytic performances of computerized decision-support systems and the ways in which the results are presented to, interpreted by, and acted on by human practitioners will affect the clinical utility of the computerized algorithm.

Beyond standalone performance, the way in which the results are presented to, interpreted by, and acted on by human practitioners in the clinical workflow will affect the ultimate clinical utility of computerized decision-support systems.

4.4.2 Study Designs to Evaluate Clinical Utility

Randomized controlled trials (RCTs) are designed as experiments with high internal validity - the ability to determine cause-effect relationships. These experiments employ comprehensive designs to control for most, if not all, sources of bias (systematic errors) by means of randomization, blinding, allocation concealment, etc. Usually, extended inclusion and exclusion criteria are used to identify a clearly defined population group of participants who would benefit from the intervention under investigation. Although the above experimental design, if correctly applied, leads to well-controlled trials with statistically credible results, their applicability to real-life practice may be questionable.

Indeed, the same characteristics that contribute to the high internal validity of a RCT (well-defined inclusion and exclusion criteria, blinding, controlled environment) can hamper its external validity, i.e. the ability to generalize the results to an extended population and clinical setting. Additionally, conducting large-scale RCTs on the clinical value of AI systems is often logistically difficult or even infeasible. In some settings, pragmatic trials, designed to show the real-world usefulness and early evidence of efficacy of a new diagnostic test in broad patient groups, offer an attractive alternative to individual randomization.

Cluster randomization (CRT), which involves groups of patients (e.g., in the same health care facility) who are randomly assigned to the same intervention (e.g., the new diagnostic test or standard care) is popular in pragmatic trials. CRTs assess outcomes aggregated at the cluster level, whereas RCTs assess individual-level outcomes. It may not be useful to use AI systems for all patients; their use could be more selective and based on patient risk factors or radiologist qualifications and capabilities. Therefore, a CRT design assessing outcomes at the cluster level (e.g., groups of patients with similar characteristics) may provide distinct advantages over individual randomization.

Many questions surround the clinical utility of AI applications (e.g., convenience of patients and physicians or efficiency in clinical workflow) and demanding a randomized design for every question of clinical utility represents an unrealistically high evidentiary standard. Instead, observational studies may be the best method to address these types of questions.

Observational studies evaluating the clinical value of AI systems can be classified as either sequential reading studies or historical comparison studies. In the sequential reading design, radiologist performance for the same patient cohort is assessed before and after the introduction of the AI system under investigation. For the historical comparison design, the performance of groups of radiologists over two periods of time is compared, and the patient cohorts and radiologists involved may not be identical for the two time periods. Observational studies are commonly used in a setting when a new diagnostic test such as an AI system for medical diagnosis has been available in clinical practice for some time after regulatory approval (e.g., US FDA approval) but evidence to prove its clinical value or to determine the recommended clinical indications is not yet available. In this case, the clinical data that have been accumulated with use of the tool in practice can be analyzed in an observational study.

Results from observational studies are often criticized for being vulnerable to confounding factors, including confounding by indications, which occurs, for instance, when the clinical indications that led to the use of a certain diagnostic or predictive AI tool also affect the patient outcome, radiologist's experience, and lack of standardization in medical care that follows an acquisition of diagnostic or predictive information. Relevant statistical procedures such as stratification and multivariable regression modeling can be used to account for confounding factors. Stratification refers to separation of patients into groups or strata according to the level of a possible confounding. This permits an analysis of each group separately, thus removing the confounding effect. Multivariable regression analysis adjusts for potential confounding factors by including them as explanatory variables in the analysis.

The assessment of long-term patient outcomes such as reduction of cancer incidence and/or cancer mortality in a cancer screening program, especially when a randomized trial is used, may not be fast enough to keep with rapid developments in computer technology such as deep learning; therefore, the AI system under investigation could become obsolete by the time a long-term RCT has been completed. A well-designed observational study can be easier and faster to conduct and yields results similar to those of randomized trials, if similar criteria are used to select patient population [254].

CHAPTER 5

Conclusions

T he recent years have seen tremendous advances in artificial intelligence, largely due to the introduction of deep learning. When it comes to applications in the healthcare domain, radiology is at the forefront of innovation with new exciting results being published on a daily basis. The prominence of machine learning at leading radiological conferences testifies to how radiologists have embraced this transformative technology. Despite some bold announcements on the existential threat that AI poses for radiology as a profession [255], many prominent radiologists and scientists are optimistic regarding its potential long term benefits [256].

Investments and research in applied AI have skyrocketed, thanks to the successes of deep learning in computer vision, natural language processing and many other fields. However, healthcare applications require extensive clinical validation, and their true clinical utility on health outcomes may not be truly assessed until they are available on the market. We have discussed many of these challenges in Chapter 4, with the hope of introducing the more technically oriented readers to the multi-faceted issues that come with moving from the research laboratories to the clinic.

At the time of writing, many AI-based applications are at the research and development stage, or have been recently cleared by regulatory agencies [155]. Hence, the actual clinical value of AI is largely speculative, and not yet sustained by strong clinical evidence. Translating technical success to meaningful clinical impact is the next great challenge, and a crucial step towards defining a successful business model for AI companies and startups. The current level of investment has been stimulated by many successful applications outside of healthcare, which are characterized by a fast pace of development and an equally short time-to-market. There is an inherent risk that comes with technological hypes: the unavoidable wave of disillusionment when they fail to deliver to heightened expectations. This risk is particularly strong with healthcare applications with long validation cycles. In this respect, recent efforts by regulatory agencies to streamline the approval of SaMDs, while ensuring their effectiveness and safety, are particularly laudable.

The current AI development model is largely data-driven, and as such the quality and quantity of data available for training are of paramount importance. Difficulties in accessing adequate datasets for training and testing are key barriers to be overcome in the near future. Research on several case studies, that we have introduced in Chapter 3, shows that we are still far from saturating the learning capacity of modern deep learning models. Ironically, medical imaging has been largely digitized for many years now, and many PACS store thousands or millions of images in a relatively well standardized format. While there are exceptions (for instance, when a new imaging modality is introduced on the market), the ultimate barriers to overcome are different: the technical and legal requirements to access the data, and the burden and cost of acquiring annotations.

The research community is striving to reduce the reliance on large scale datasets. There is abundant research aimed at alleviating the limited dataset size problem in medical imaging, or alternatively at leveraging unlabeled large scale datasets. Many of these research endeavors, including advances in transfer and multi-task learning, data augmentation and semi-supervised learning from retrospective data, have been described in Chapter 2, and if successful will largely reduce the amount of data necessary to train new applications. Other possibilities, such as active learning, are discussed in recent reviews [32]. While not included in this concise introduction, privacy-aware, distributed training algorithms are another emerging technique which may alleviate the need to transfer sensitive data by sharing model parameters instead.

At the same time, we need continued efforts to facilitate the access to medical data for the research and industry communities. The ethical need to protect people's privacy and regulate access to personal data needs to be balanced with the potential benefits of using such data not only for basic research, but also to develop new technology. This balance is difficult to navigate, as demonstrated by high profile legal cases such as the debated partnership between Google DeepMind and the Royal Free London NHS Foundation

Trust [257]. This debate is more relevant than ever with the adoption of the new General Data Protection Regulation (GDPR) in the European Union. In the current global race to AI development, many worry that countries with more permissive privacy regulations, such as China, may acquire a substantial long term advantage [258, 259]. It is conceivable that each country will tackle this issue differently, depending on the organization of its healthcare system and the prevalance of private or public-based institutions. In Europe, there is an emerging awareness of the potentiality of imaging biobanks to balance these delicate requirements [260, 261]. The diffusion of competitive challenges and public datasets will further foster reproducible and open innovation [32].

When talking about data quality, the first issue that comes to mind within the medical domain is the quality of annotations by expert radiologists. However, the presence of potential biases or confounding factors, as discussed in Chapter 4, is equally important. Both conventional machine learning and deep learning are not able to distinguish clinically relevant differences from biases in the training data, as they mainly work by statistical association which may arise in data collection regardless of the underlying true causal mechanisms. Important clinical and also ethical implications arise when such models are deployed to the clinic, especially for ethnic minorities and in general sub-populations which may be under-represented in current clinical systems [262].

AI technology is evolving rapidly, and it would be impossible to list here all directions for future improvement. However, we wish to point the reader's attention in particular to the issue of self-learning and adaptive systems. At the time of writing, healthcare AI applications, albeit sophisticated, are deployed as static, "locked" systems which can be updated but do not learn automatically. We envision an increased interest in researching self-supervised and active learning systems that can evolve over time as new training data becomes available, perhaps even specializing on the specific population or acquisition protocol of each clinical center. We introduce in Chapter 4 the important issue of how regulatory agencies are working to adapt regulatory frameworks in this sense.

Another obstacle related to the widespread adoption of AI in healthcare is the (perceived) lack of transparency of deep learning based models. Partly, these difficulties stem from our limited theoretical understanding of the practical success of deep learning, which despite remarkable progress is still far from complete. History offers many similar examples when engineering and invention have preceded the scientific understanding of the underlying principles that make the invention work.

Besides concerns related to possible system failures and their effect on patient care, lack of transparency may be particularly dangerous when coupled with dataset biases, which may be undetected if the learning system is opaque. There is an increasing interest in making AI systems interpretable, transparent and explainable, stimulated also by the larger issue of algorithmic fairness and the emergence of regulatory requirements such as the "right to explanation" envisioned by the GDPR [32, 263, 264]. In artificial vision applications, this goal is at the state-of-the-art mostly achieved through visual explanations, which we have briefly discussed in Chapter 2. However, we envision new exciting developments in the field of explainable AI, where interpretability and what it means for final users and researchers remain the subjects of lively debate. Ultimately, however, our willingness to rely on AI in healthcare, especially if and when automation will become part of the radiology workflow, will depend on winning the trust of users and society at large. Trust in automation is a complex, multi-faceted issue, which can certainly benefit from the ability to understand, at least to a certain extent, how an AI system works. However, we must not forget that long term trust also depends, to a large extent, on the perceived performance and reliability of the system; we believe that, with or without advances in explainability, clinical performance will be the major factor driving AI uptake in the radiological field. For this reason, given the incredible pace of development witnessed in these years and of which the reader has hopefully had a glimpse throughout this book, our hopes are high.

Bibliography

[1] Pamela McCorduck. *Machines Who Think*. W. H. Freeman & Co., New York, 1979.

[2] Computer AI passes Turing test in 'world first'. https://www.bbc.com/news/technology-27762088. Accessed: 2019-06-09.

[3] Parnian Afshar, Arash Mohammadi, Konstantinos N. Plataniotis, Anastasia Oikonomou, and Habib Benali. From hand-crafted to deep learning-based cancer radiomics: Challenges and opportunities. *CoRR*, abs/1808.07954, 2018.

[4] Anil Jain and Douglas Zongker. Feature selection: Evaluation, application, and small sample performance. *IEEE Trans. Pattern Anal. Mach. Intell.*, 19(2):153–158, 1997.

[5] Isabelle Guyon and André Elisseeff. An introduction to variable and feature selection. *Journal of Machine Learning Research*, 3(Mar):1157–1182, 2003.

[6] Jack Sklansky. Image segmentation and feature extraction. *IEEE Transactions on Systems, Man, and Cybernetics*, 8(4):237–247, 1978.

[7] Jiawei Han, Micheline Kamber, and Jian Pei. *Data Mining: Concepts and Techniques (3rd ed.)*. Morgan Kaufmann, Boston, 2011.

[8] Ira Cohen, Fabio G. Cozman, Nicu Sebe, Marcelo C. Cirelo, and Thomas S. Huang. Semisupervised learning of classifiers: Theory, algorithms, and their application to human-computer interaction. *IEEE Trans. Pattern Anal. Mach. Intell.*, 26(12):1553–1567, December 2004.

[9] Shai Shalev-Shwartz and Shai Ben-David. *Understanding Machine Learning: From Theory to Algorithms*. Cambridge University Press, 2014.

[10] Christopher M. Bishop. *Pattern Recognition and Machine Learning* (Information Science and Statistics Series). Springer, Berlin, 2006.

[11] Richard O. Duda, Peter E. Hart, and David G. Stork. *Pattern Classification (2nd ed.)*. Wiley-Interscience, New York, 2000.

[12] Brian D. Ripley and N. L. Hjort. *Pattern Recognition and Neural Networks*. Cambridge University Press, New York, 1995.

[13] Nir Friedman, Dan Geiger, and Moises Goldszmidt. Bayesian network classifiers. *Machine Learning*, 29(2-3):131–163, 1997.

[14] Geoffrey I. Webb, Janice R. Boughton, and Zhihai Wang. Not so naive Bayes: Aggregating one-dependence estimators. *Machine Learning*, 58(1):5–24, 2005.

[15] Yoav Freund and Robert E. Schapire. Large margin classification using the perceptron algorithm. *Machine Learning*, 37(3):277–296, 1999.

[16] T. J. Cole. Applied logistic regression. In *Statistics in Medicine*. John Wiley & Sons, New York, 1991.

[17] Corinna Cortes and Vladimir Vapnik. Support-vector networks. *Machine Learning*, 20(3):273–297, 1995.

[18] Christopher J. C. Burges. A tutorial on support vector machines for pattern recognition. *Data Mining and Knowledge Discovery*, 2:121–167, 1998.

[19] Leo Breiman. Random forests. *Machine Learning*, 45(1):5–32, 2001.

[20] Tin Kam Ho. The random subspace method for constructing decision forests. *IEEE Transactions on Pattern Analysis and Machine Intelligence*, 20(8):832–844, 1998.

[21] Yali Amit and Donald Geman. Shape quantization and recognition with randomized trees. *Neural Comput.*, 9(7):1545–1588, 1997.

[22] Daniel J. Amit. *Modeling Brain Function—The World of Attractor Neural Networks*. Cambridge University Press, New York, 1989.

[23] Christopher M. Bishop. *Neural Networks for Pattern Recognition*. Oxford University Press, New York, 1995.

[24] Jürgen Schmidhuber. Deep learning in neural networks: An overview. *Neural Networks*, 61:85–117, 2015.

[25] Ian Goodfellow, Yoshua Bengio, and Aaron Courville. *Deep Learning*. MIT Press, 2016. http://www.deeplearning book.org.

[26] Yann LeCun, Yoshua Bengio, and Geoffrey Hinton. Deep learning. *Nature*, 521(7553):436, 2015.

[27] Yann LeCun, Léon Bottou, Yoshua Bengio, Patrick Haffner, et al. Gradient-based learning applied to document recognition. *Proceedings of the IEEE*, 86(11):2278–2324, 1998.

[28] Geert Litjens, Thijs Kooi, Babak Ehteshami Bejnordi, Arnaud Arindra Adiyoso Setio, Francesco Ciompi, Mohsen Ghafoorian, Jeroen Awm Van Der Laak, Bram Van Ginneken, and Clara I. Sánchez. A survey on deep learning in medical image analysis. *Medical Image Analysis*, 42:60–88, 2017.

[29] Karen Simonyan and Andrew Zisserman. Very deep convolutional networks for large-scale image recognition. *arXiv preprint arXiv:1409.1556*, 2014.

[30] Jason Yosinski, Jeff Clune, Yoshua Bengio, and Hod Lipson. How transferable are features in deep neural networks? In *Advances in neural information processing systems*, 2014, pages 3320–3328.

[31] Fred Matthew Hohman, Minsuk Kahng, Robert Pienta, and Duen Horng Chau. Visual analytics in deep learning: An interrogative survey for the next frontiers. *IEEE Transactions on Visualization and Computer Graphics*, 2018.

[32] Berkman Sahiner, Aria Pezeshk, Lubomir M. Hadjiiski, Xiaosong Wang, Karen Drukker, Kenny H. Cha, Ronald M. Summers, and Maryellen L. Giger. Deep learning in medical imaging and radiation therapy. *Medical Physics*, 46(1):e1–e36, 2019.

[33] Sara Sabour, Nicholas Frosst, and Geoffrey E. Hinton. Dynamic routing between capsules. In *Advances in Neural Information Processing Systems*, 2017, pages 3856–3866.

[34] Christian Eggert, Stephan Brehm, Anton Winschel, Dan Zecha, and Rainer Lienhart. A closer look: Small object detection in faster R-CNN. In *Proceedings of IEEE International Conference on Multimedia and Expo*, IEEE, 2017, pages 421–426.

[35] Alfredo Canziani, Adam Paszke, and Eugenio Culurciello. An analysis of deep neural network models for practical applications. *arXiv preprint arXiv:1605.07678*, 2016.

[36] Olga Russakovsky, Jia Deng, Hao Su, Jonathan Krause, Sanjeev Satheesh, Sean Ma, Zhiheng Huang, Andrej Karpathy, Aditya Khosla, Michael Bernstein, et al. Imagenet large scale visual recognition challenge. *International Journal of Computer Vision*, 115(3):211–252, 2015.

[37] Simon Kornblith, Jonathon Shlens, and Quoc V. Le. Do better imagenet models transfer better? In *Proceedings of Conference on Computer Vision and Pattern Recognition*, IEEE, 2019, pages 2661–2671.

[38] Kaiming He, Xiangyu Zhang, Shaoqing Ren, and Jian Sun. Deep residual learning for image recognition. In *Proceedings of Conference on Computer Vision and Pattern Recognition*, IEEE, 2016, pages 770–778.

[39] C. Szegedy, Wei Liu, Yangqing Jia, P. Sermanet, S. Reed, D. Anguelov, D. Erhan, V. Vanhoucke, and A. Rabinovich. Going deeper with convolutions. In *2015 IEEE Conference on Computer Vision and Pattern Recognition*, IEEE, 2015, pages 1–9.

[40] Christian Szegedy, Sergey Ioffe, and Vincent Vanhoucke. Inception-v4, inception-resnet and the impact of residual connections on learning. In *Thirty-First AAAI Conference on Artificial Intelligence*, 2017.

[41] Gao Huang, Zhuang Liu, Laurens Van Der Maaten, and Kilian Q. Weinberger. Densely connected convolutional networks. In *Proceedings of Conference on Computer Vision and Pattern Recognition*, IEEE, 2017, pages 4700–4708.

[42] Sepp Hochreiter and Jürgen Schmidhuber. Long short-term memory. *Neural Computation*, 9(8):1735–1780, 1997.

[43] Ling Zhang, Le Lu, Robert M. Zhu, Mohammadhadi Bagheri, Ronald M. Summers, and Jianhua Yao. Spatial-temporal convolutional LSTMs for tumor growth prediction by learning 4D longitudinal patient data. *arXiv preprint arXiv:1902.08716*, 2019.

[44] Ashish Vaswani, Noam Shazeer, Niki Parmar, Jakob Uszkoreit, Llion Jones, Aidan N Gomez, Łukasz Kaiser, and Illia Polosukhin. Attention is all you need. In *Advances in neural information processing systems*, 2017, pages 5998–6008.

[45] Fei Wang, Mengqing Jiang, Chen Qian, Shuo Yang, Cheng Li, Honggang Zhang, Xiaogang Wang, and Xiaoou Tang. Residual attention network for image classification. In *Proceedings of Conference on Computer Vision and Pattern Recognition*, IEEE, 2017, pages 3156–3164.

[46] John Pavlopoulos, Vasiliki Kougia, and Ion Androutsopoulos. A survey on biomedical image captioning. In *Proceedings of the Second Workshop on Shortcomings in Vision and Language*, pages 26–36, 2019.

[47] Ewoud Pons, Loes M.M. Braun, M.G. Myriam Hunink, and Jan A. Kors. Natural language processing in radiology: a systematic review. *Radiology*, 279(2):329–343, 2016.

[48] Ke Yan, Xiaosong Wang, Le Lu, and Ronald M. Summers. DeepLesion: automated mining of large-scale lesion annotations and universal lesion detection with deep learning. *Journal of Medical Imaging*, 5(3):036501, 2018.

[49] Dezső Ribli, Anna Horváth, Zsuzsa Unger, Péter Pollner, and István Csabai. Detecting and classifying lesions in mammograms with deep learning. *Scientific Reports*, 8(1):4165, 2018.

[50] Jonas Teuwen, Sil van de Leemput, Albert Gubern-Mérida, Alejandro Rodriguez-Ruiz, Ritse Mann, and Babak Ehteshami Bejnordi. Soft tissue lesion detection in mammography using deep neural networks for object detection. 2018.

[51] Shaoqing Ren, Kaiming He, Ross Girshick, and Jian Sun. Faster R-CNN: Towards real-time object detection with region proposal networks. In *Advances in Neural Information Processing Systems*, 2015, pages 91–99.

[52] Joseph Redmon, Santosh Divvala, Ross Girshick, and Ali Farhadi. You only look once: Unified, real-time object detection. In *Proceedings of Conference on Computer Vision and Pattern Recognition*, IEEE, 2016, pages 779–788.

[53] Tsung-Yi Lin, Priya Goyal, Ross Girshick, Kaiming He, and Piotr Dollár. Focal loss for dense object detection. In *Proceedings of International Conference on Computer Vision*, IEEE, 2017, pages 2980–2988.

[54] Krzysztof Geras, Stacey Wolfson, S. Gene Kim, Linda Moy, and Kyunghyun Cho. High-resolution breast cancer screening with multi-view deep convolutional neural networks. *arXiv preprint arXiv:1703.07047*, 2017.

[55] Jameson Merkow, Robert Lufkin, Kim Nguyen, Stefano Soatto, Zhuowen Tu, and Andrea Vedaldi. DeepRadiology-Net: radiologist level pathology detection in CT head images. *arXiv preprint arXiv:1711.09313*, 2017.

[56] David B. Larson, Matthew C. Chen, Matthew P. Lungren, Safwan S. Halabi, Nicholas V. Stence, and Curtis P. Langlotz. Performance of a deep-learning neural network model in assessing skeletal maturity on pediatric hand radiographs. *Radiology*, 287(1):313–322, 2017.

[57] Pranav Rajpurkar, Jeremy Irvin, Kaylie Zhu, Brandon Yang, Hershel Mehta, Tony Duan, Daisy Ding, Aarti Bagul, Curtis Langlotz, Katie Shpanskaya, et al. CheXNet: Radiologist-level pneumonia detection on chest X-rays with deep learning. *arXiv preprint arXiv:1711.05225*, 2017.

[58] Olaf Ronneberger, Philipp Fischer, and Thomas Brox. U-net: Convolutional networks for biomedical image segmentation. In *International Conference on Medical Image Computing and Computer-Assisted Intervention*, pages 234–241. Springer, 2015.

[59] Fausto Milletari, Nassir Navab, and Seyed-Ahmad Ahmadi. V-net: Fully convolutional neural networks for volumetric medical image segmentation. In *Proceedings of 4th International Conference on 3D Vision*, IEEE, 2016, pages 565–571.

[60] Liang-Chieh Chen, George Papandreou, Iasonas Kokkinos, Kevin Murphy, and Alan L. Yuille. Deeplab: Semantic image segmentation with deep convolutional nets, atrous convolution, and fully connected CRFs. *IEEE Transactions on Pattern Analysis and Machine Intelligence*, 40(4):834–848, 2017.

[61] Wei Zha, Sean B. Fain, Mark L. Schiebler, Michael D. Evans, Scott K. Nagle, and Fang Liu. Deep convolutional neural networks with multiplane consensus labeling for lung function quantification using UTE proton MRI. *Journal of Magnetic Resonance Imaging*, 2019.

[62] Samitha Herath, Mehrtash Harandi, and Fatih Porikli. Going deeper into action recognition: A survey. *Image and Vision Computing*, 60:4–21, 2017.

[63] Ling Zhang, Le Lu, Ronald M. Summers, Electron Kebebew, and Jianhua Yao. Convolutional invasion and expansion networks for tumor growth prediction. *Transactions on Medical Imaging*, 37(2):638–648, 2017.

[64] Philip Teare, Michael Fishman, Oshra Benzaquen, Eyal Toledano, and Eldad Elnekave. Malignancy detection on mammography using dual deep convolutional neural networks and genetically discovered false color input enhancement. *J. Digital Imaging*, 30(4):499–505, 2017.

[65] Konstantinos Kamnitsas, Christian Ledig, Virginia F.J. Newcombe, Joanna P. Simpson, Andrew D. Kane, David K. Menon, Daniel Rueckert, and Ben Glocker. Efficient multiscale 3D CNN with fully connected CRF for accurate brain lesion segmentation. *Medical Image Analysis*, 36:61–78, 2017.

[66] Shin Hoo-Chang, Holger R. Roth, Mingchen Gao, Le Lu, Ziyue Xu, Isabella Nogues, Jianhua Yao, Daniel Mollura, and Ronald M. Summers. Deep convolutional neural networks for computer-aided detection: CNN architectures, dataset characteristics and transfer learning. *IEEE Transactions on Medical Imaging*, 35(5):1285, 2016.

[67] Heung-Il Suk, Seong-Whan Lee, Dinggang Shen, Alzheimer's Disease Neuroimaging Initiative, et al. Hierarchical feature representation and multimodal fusion with deep learning for AD/MCI diagnosis. *NeuroImage*, 101:569–582, 2014.

[68] Thijs Kooi and Nico Karssemeijer. Deep learning of symmetrical discrepancies for computer-aided detection of mammographic masses. In *Medical Imaging 2017: Computer-Aided Diagnosis*, volume 10134, page 101341J, 2017.

[69] Jiquan Ngiam, Aditya Khosla, Mingyu Kim, Juhan Nam, Honglak Lee, and Andrew Y. Ng. Multimodal deep learning. In *Proceedings of 28th international conference on machine learning*, 2011, pages 689–696.

[70] Ian Goodfellow, Jean Pouget-Abadie, Mehdi Mirza, Bing Xu, David Warde-Farley, Sherjil Ozair, Aaron Courville, and Yoshua Bengio. Generative adversarial nets. In *Advances in Neural Information Processing Systems*, pages 2672–2680, 2014.

[71] Xin Yi, Ekta Walia, and Paul Babyn. Generative adversarial network in medical imaging: a review. *Medical image analysis*, 2019, 101552.

[72] Salome Kazeminia, Christoph Baur, Arjan Kuijper, Bram van Ginneken, Nassir Navab, Shadi Albarqouni, and Anirban Mukhopadhyay. GANs for medical image analysis. *arXiv preprint arXiv:1809.06222*, 2018.

[73] Jun-Yan Zhu, Taesung Park, Phillip Isola, and Alexei A. Efros. Unpaired image-to-image translation using cycle-consistent adversarial networks. In *Proceedings of International Conference on Computer Vision*, IEEE, 2017, pages 2223–2232.

[74] Hoo-Chang Shin, Neil A. Tenenholtz, Jameson K. Rogers, Christopher G. Schwarz, Matthew L. Senjem, Jeffrey L. Gunter, Katherine P. Andriole, and Mark Michalski. Medical image synthesis for data augmentation and anonymization using generative adversarial networks. In *International Workshop on Simulation and Synthesis in Medical Imaging*, pages 1–11. Springer, 2018.

[75] Yoshua Bengio. Practical recommendations for gradient-based training of deep architectures. In *Neural Networks: Tricks of the Trade*, pages 437–478. Springer, 2012.

[76] Jason Brownlee. Machine learning mastery. http://machine learningmastery.com/discover-feature-engineering-howtoengineer-features-and-how-to-getgood-at-it, 2014. Accessed: 2019-07-20.

[77] Adrian Rosenbrock. Deep learning for computer vision with Python. https://www.pyimagesearch.com/deep-learn ing-computer-vision-python-book/. Accessed: 2019-07-20.

[78] Francois Chollet. Deep learning with Python. Safari Tech Books Online. Manning, Shelter Island, New York, 2018.

[79] Léon Bottou, Frank E. Curtis, and Jorge Nocedal. Optimization methods for large-scale machine learning. *Siam Review*, 60(2):223–311, 2018.

[80] Leslie N. Smith. Cyclical learning rates for training neural networks. In *2017 IEEE Winter Conference on Applications of Computer Vision*, IEEE, 2017, pages 464–472.

[81] James Bergstra and Yoshua Bengio. Random search for hyper-parameter optimization. *Journal of Machine Learning Research*, 13:281–305, 2012.

[82] Kenneth O. Stanley and Risto Miikkulainen. Evolving neural networks through augmenting topologies. *Evolutionary Computing*, 10(2):99–127, 2002.

[83] Risto Miikkulainen, Jason Liang, Elliot Meyerson, Aditya Rawal, Dan Fink, Olivier Francon, Bala Raju, Arshak Navruzyan, Nigel Duffy, and Babak Hodjat. Evolving deep neural networks. In *Artificial Intelligence in the Age of Neural Networks and Brain Computing*, pp. 293–312. Academic Press.

[84] Ian Dewancker, Michael McCourt, Scott Clark, Patrick Hayes, Alexandra Johnson, and George Ke. A stratified analysis of Bayesian optimization methods. *arXiv preprint arXiv:1603.09441*, 2016.

[85] Ian Dewancker, Michael McCourt, and Scott Clark. Bayesian optimization for machine learning: A practical guidebook. *arXiv preprint arXiv:1612.04858*, 2016.

[86] Jialei Wang, Scott C. Clark, Eric Liu, and Peter I. Frazier. Parallel Bayesian global optimization of expensive functions. *arXiv preprint arXiv:1602.05149*, 2016.

[87] E. Angelie, P.J.H. de Koning, M.G. Danilouchkine, H.C. Van Assen, G. Koning, R.J. Van Der Geest, and J.H.C. Reiber. Optimizing the automatic segmentation of the left ventricle in magnetic resonance images. *Medical Physics*, 32(2):369–375, 2005.

[88] Juan Wang, Robert M. Nishikawa, and Yongyi Yang. Global detection approach for clustered microcalcifications in mammograms using a deep learning network. *Journal of Medical Imaging*, 4(2):024501–024501, 2017.

[89] Lia Morra, Nunzia Coccia, and Tania Cerquitelli. Optimization of computer aided detection systems: An evolutionary approach. *Expert Systems With Applications*, 100:145–156, 2018.

[90] George Teodoro, Tahsin M. Kurç, Luís FR Taveira, Alba C.M.A. Melo, Yi Gao, Jun Kong, and Joel H. Saltz. Algorithm sensitivity analysis and parameter tuning for tissue image segmentation pipelines. *Bioinformatics*, 33(7):1064–1072, 2016.

[91] Alex Krizhevsky, Ilya Sutskever, and Geoffrey E. Hinton. Imagenet classification with deep convolutional neural networks. In *Advances in Neural Information Processing Systems*, pages 1097–1105, 2012.

[92] Ekin D. Cubuk, Barret Zoph, Dandelion Mane, Vijay Vasudevan, and Quoc V. Le. Autoaugment: Learning augmentation policies from data. *arXiv preprint arXiv:1805.09501*, 2018.

[93] Amy Zhao, Guha Balakrishnan, Fredo Durand, John V. Guttag, and Adrian V. Dalca. Data augmentation using learned transformations for one-shot medical image segmentation. In *Proceedings of Conference on Computer Vision and Pattern Recognition*, IEEE, 2019, pages 8543–8553.

[94] Joseph Paul Cohen, Margaux Luck, and Sina Honari. Distribution matching losses can hallucinate features in medical image translation. In *International Conference on Medical Image Computing and Computer-Assisted Intervention*, pages 529–536. Springer, 2018.

[95] Wouter M. Kouw, Marco Loog, Lambertus W. Bartels, and Adriënne M. Mendrik. MR acquisition-invariant representation learning. *arXiv preprint arXiv:1709.07944*, 2017.

[96] Veronika Cheplygina, Marleen de Bruijne, and Josien P.W. Pluim. Not-so-supervised: a survey of semi-supervised, multi-instance, and transfer learning in medical image analysis. *Medical Image Analysis*, 2019.

[97] Amir R. Zamir, Alexander Sax, William Shen, Leonidas J. Guibas, Jitendra Malik, and Silvio Savarese. Taskonomy: Disentangling task transfer learning. In *Proceedings of Conference on Computer Vision and Pattern Recognition*, IEEE, 2018, pages 3712–3722.

[98] Sinno Jialin Pan and Qiang Yang. A survey on transfer learning. *IEEE Transactions on Knowledge and Data Engineering*, 22(10):1345–1359, 2009.

[99] Ravi K. Samala, Heang-Ping Chan, Lubomir Hadjiiski, Mark A. Helvie, Caleb D. Richter, and Kenny H. Cha. Breast cancer diagnosis in digital breast tomosynthesis: Effects of training sample size on multi-stage transfer learning using deep neural nets. *IEEE Transactions on Medical Imaging*, 2018.

[100] Nima Tajbakhsh, Jae Y. Shin, Suryakanth R. Gurudu, R. Todd Hurst, Christopher B. Kendall, Michael B. Gotway, and Jianming Liang. Convolutional neural networks for medical image analysis: Full training or fine tuning? *IEEE Transactions on Medical Imaging*, 35(5):1299–1312, 2016.

[101] Veronika Cheplygina. Cats or CAT scans: transfer learning from natural or medical image source datasets? *Current Opinions in Biomedical Engineering*, 2019.

[102] Afonso Menegola, Michel Fornaciali, Ramon Pires, Flávia Vasques Bittencourt, Sandra Avila, and Eduardo Valle. Knowledge transfer for melanoma screening with deep learning. In *Proceedings of 14th International Symposium on Biomedical Imaging*, IEEE, 2017, pages 297–300.

[103] Francesco Ponzio, Gianvito Urgese, Elisa Ficarra, and Santa Di Cataldo. Dealing with lack of training data for convolutional neural networks: The case of digital pathology. *Electronics*, 8(3):256, 2019.

[104] Eduardo Ribeiro, Andreas Uhl, Georg Wimmer, and Michael Häfner. Exploring deep learning and transfer learning for colonic polyp classification. *Computational and Mathematical Methods in Medicine*, 2016, 2016.

[105] Kenny H. Cha, Lubomir M. Hadjiiski, Heang-Ping Chan, Ravi K. Samala, Richard H. Cohan, Elaine M. Caoili, Chintana Paramagul, Ajjai Alva, and Alon Z. Weizer. Bladder cancer treatment response assessment using deep learning in CT with transfer learning. In *Medical Imaging 2017: Computer-Aided Diagnosis*, volume 10134, page 1013404, 2017.

[106] Hak Gu Kim, Yeoreum Choi, and Yong Man Ro. Modality-bridge transfer learning for medical image classification. In *Proceedings of 10th International Congress on Image and Signal Processing, Biomedical Engineering and Informatics*, IEEE, 2017, pages 1–5.

[107] Gabriela Csurka. A comprehensive survey on domain adaptation for visual applications. In *Domain Adaptation in Computer Vision Applications*, pages 1–35. Springer, 2017.

[108] Gabriele Angeletti, Barbara Caputo, and Tatiana Tommasi. Adaptive deep learning through visual domain localization. In *2018 IEEE International Conference on Robotics and Automation (ICRA)*, pages 7135–7142, 2018.

[109] Sailesh Conjeti, Amin Katouzian, Abhijit Guha Roy, Loïc Peter, Debdoot Sheet, Stéphane Carlier, Andrew Laine, and Nassir Navab. Supervised domain adaptation of decision forests: Transfer of models trained in vitro for in vivo intravascular ultrasound tissue characterization. *Medical Image Analysis*, 32:1–17, 2016.

[110] Mohsen Ghafoorian, Alireza Mehrtash, Tina Kapur, Nico Karssemeijer, Elena Marchiori, Mehran Pesteie, Charles RG Guttmann, Frank-Erik de Leeuw, Clare M. Tempany, Bram van Ginneken, et al. Transfer learning for domain adaptation in MRI: Application in brain lesion segmentation. In *International Conference on Medical Image Computing and Computer-Assisted Intervention*, pages 516–524. Springer, 2017.

[111] Christian Wachinger, Martin Reuter, Alzheimer's Disease Neuroimaging Initiative, et al. Domain adaptation for Alzheimer's disease diagnostics. *Neuroimage*, 139:470–479, 2016.

[112] Faisal Mahmood, Richard Chen, and Nicholas J. Durr. Unsupervised reverse domain adaptation for synthetic medical images via adversarial training. *IEEE Transactions on Medical Imaging*, 37(12):2572–2581, 2018.

[113] Cheng Chen, Qi Dou, Hao Chen, and Pheng-Ann Heng. Semantic-aware generative adversarial nets for unsupervised domain adaptation in chest x-ray segmentation. In *International Workshop on Machine Learning in Medical Imaging*, pages 143–151. Springer, 2018.

[114] Yue Huang, Han Zheng, Chi Liu, Xinghao Ding, and Gustavo K. Rohde. Epithelium-stroma classification via convolutional neural networks and unsupervised domain adaptation in histopathological images. *IEEE Journal of Biomedical and Health Informatics*, 21(6):1625–1632, 2017.

[115] Yuankai Huo, Zhoubing Xu, Shunxing Bao, Albert Assad, Richard G. Abramson, and Bennett A. Landman. Adversarial synthesis learning enables segmentation without target modality ground truth. In *15th International Symposium on Biomedical Imaging (ISBI 2018)*, IEEE, 2018, pages 1217–1220.

[116] Agisilaos Chartsias, Thomas Joyce, Rohan Dharmakumar, and Sotirios A. Tsaftaris. Adversarial image synthesis for unpaired multi-modal cardiac data. In *International Workshop on Simulation and Synthesis in Medical Imaging*, pages 3–13. Springer, 2017.

[117] Jue Jiang, Yu-Chi Hu, Neelam Tyagi, Pengpeng Zhang, Andreas Rimner, Gig S. Mageras, Joseph O. Deasy, and Harini Veeraraghavan. Tumor-aware, adversarial domain adaptation from CT to MRI for lung cancer segmentation. In *International Conference on Medical Image Computing and Computer-Assisted Intervention*, pages 777–785. Springer, 2018.

[118] Pim Moeskops, Jelmer M. Wolterink, Bas H.M. van der Velden, Kenneth G.A. Gilhuijs, Tim Leiner, Max A. Viergever, and Ivana Išgum. Deep learning for multi-task medical image segmentation in multiple modalities. In *Proceedings of International Conference on Medical Image Computing and Computer-Assisted Intervention*, Springer, 2016, pages 478–486.

[119] Gabriel Maicas, Andrew P. Bradley, Jacinto C. Nascimento, Ian Reid, and Gustavo Carneiro. Training medical image analysis systems like radiologists. In *Proceedings of International Conference on Medical Image Computing and Computer-Assisted Intervention*, pages 546–554. Springer, 2018.

[120] Marc D. Kohli, Ronald M. Summers, and J. Raymond Geis. Medical image data and datasets in the era of machine learning—whitepaper from the 2016 C-MIMI meeting dataset session. *Journal of Digital Imaging*, 30(4):392–399, 2017.

[121] Nima Tajbakhsh, Yufei Hu, Junli Cao, Xingjian Yan, Yi Xiao, Yong Lu, Jianming Liang, Demetri Terzopoulos, and Xiaowei Ding. Surrogate supervision for medical image analysis: Effective deep learning from limited quantities of labeled data. *arXiv preprint arXiv:1901.08707*, 2019.

[122] Silvia Bucci, Antonio D'Innocente, and Tatiana Tommasi. Tackling partial domain adaptation with self-supervision. *arXiv preprint arXiv:1906.05199*, 2019.

[123] Amir Jamaludin, Timor Kadir, and Andrew Zisserman. Self-supervised learning for spinal MRIs. In *Deep Learning in Medical Image Analysis and Multimodal Learning for Clinical Decision Support*. Springer, 2017, pages 294–302.

[124] Hoo-Chang Shin, Le Lu, Lauren Kim, Ari Seff, Jianhua Yao, and Ronald M. Summers. Interleaved text/image deep mining on a very large-scale radiology database. In *Proceedings of conference on computer vision and pattern recognition*, IEEE, 2015, pages 1090–1099.

[125] Lia Morra, Daniela Sacchetto, Manuela Durando, Silvano Agliozzo, Luca Alessandro Carbonaro, Silvia Delsanto, Barbara Pesce, Diego Persano, Giovanna Mariscotti, Vincenzo Marra, et al. Breast cancer: computer-aided detection with digital breast tomosynthesis. *Radiology*, 277(1):56–63, 2015.

[126] Adrian P. Brady. Error and discrepancy in radiology: inevitable or avoidable? *Insights into Imaging*, 8(1):171–182, 2017.

[127] Daniela Sacchetto, Lia Morra, Silvano Agliozzo, Daniela Bernardi, Tomas Björklund, Beniamino Brancato, Patrizia Bravetti, Luca A Carbonaro, Loredana Correale, Carmen Fantò, et al. Mammographic density: comparison of visual assessment with fully automatic calculation on a multivendor dataset. *European Radiology*, 26(1):175–183, 2016.

[128] Samuel G. Armato III, Geoffrey McLennan, Luc Bidaut, Michael F. McNitt-Gray, Charles R. Meyer, Anthony P. Reeves, Binsheng Zhao, Denise R. Aberle, Claudia I. Henschke, Eric A. Hoffman, et al. The Lung Image Database Consortium (LIDC) and Image Database Resource Initiative (IDRI): a completed reference database of lung nodules on CT scans. *Medical Physics*, 38(2):915–931, 2011.

[129] Kunio Doi. Current status and future potential of computer-aided diagnosis in medical imaging. *The British Journal of Radiology*, 78(suppl_1):s3–s19, 2005.

[130] Bram van Ginneken, Cornelia M. Schaefer-Prokop, and Mathias Prokop. Computer-aided diagnosis: how to move from the laboratory to the clinic. *Radiology*, 261(3):719–732, 2011.

[131] Mehmet Günhan Ertosun and Daniel L. Rubin. Automated grading of gliomas using deep learning in digital pathology images: A modular approach with ensemble of convolutional neural networks. In *AMIA Annual Symposium Proceedings*, volume 2015, page 1899. American Medical Informatics Association, 2015.

[132] Massimo Salvi and Filippo Molinari. Multi-tissue and multi-scale approach for nuclei segmentation in H&E stained images. *Biomedical Engineering Online*, 17(1):89, 2018.

[133] Massimo Salvi, Filippo Molinari, Natalia Dogliani, and Martino Bosco. Automatic discrimination of neoplastic epithelium and stromal response in breast carcinoma. *Computers in Biology and Medicine*, 110:8–14, 2019.

[134] Zhuo Zhang, Ruchir Srivastava, Huiying Liu, Xiangyu Chen, Lixin Duan, Damon Wing Kee Wong, Chee Keong Kwoh, Tien Yin Wong, and Jiang Liu. A survey on computer aided diagnosis for ocular diseases. *BMC Medical Informatics and Decision Making*, 14(1):80, 2014.

[135] Varun Gulshan, Lily Peng, Marc Coram, Martin C. Stumpe, Derek Wu, Arunachalam Narayanaswamy, Subhashini Venugopalan, Kasumi Widner, Tom Madams, Jorge Cuadros, Ramasamy Kim, Rajiv Raman, Philip C. Nelson, Jessica L. Mega, and Dale R. Webster. Development and validation of a deep learning algorithm for detection of diabetic retinopathy in retinal fundus photographs. *JAMA*, 316(22):2402–2410, 2016.

[136] Harry Pratt, Frans Coenen, Deborah M. Broadbent, Simon P Harding, and Yalin Zheng. Convolutional neural networks for diabetic retinopathy. *Procedia Computer Science*, 90:200–205, 2016.

[137] Holger A. Haenssle, Christine Fink, R. Schneiderbauer, Ferdinand Toberer, Timo Buhl, A. Blum, A. Kalloo, A. Ben Hadj Hassen, L. Thomas, A. Enk, et al. Man against machine: diagnostic performance of a deep learning convolutional neural network for dermoscopic melanoma recognition in comparison to 58 dermatologists. *Annals of Oncology*, 29(8):1836–1842, 2018.

[138] Andre Esteva, Brett Kuprel, Roberto A. Novoa, Justin Ko, Susan M. Swetter, Helen M. Blau, and Sebastian Thrun. Dermatologist-level classification of skin cancer with deep neural networks. *Nature*, 542(7639):115, 2017.

[139] Mauricio Goihman-Yahr. Wound measurement by computer-aided design (CAD): a practical approach for software utility. *International Journal of Dermatology*, 37(9):714–715, 1998.

[140] Ruikai Zhang, Yali Zheng, Tony Wing Chung Mak, Ruoxi Yu, Sunny H. Wong, James Y.W. Lau, and Carmen C.Y. Poon. Automatic detection and classification of colorectal polyps by transferring low-level CNN features from nonmedical domain. *IEEE Journal of Biomedical and Health Informatics*, 21(1):41–47, 2016.

[141] Charles E. Kahn Jr. Artificial intelligence in radiology: decision support systems. *Radiographics*, 14(4):849–861, 1994.

[142] Anil K. Jain. *Fundamentals of Digital Image Processing*. Prentice Hall, Englewood Cliffs, NJ, 1989.

[143] Rafael C. Gonzalez and E. Richard Woods. *Digital Image Processing*. Prentice Hall, New York, 2002.

[144] Geoff Dougherty. *Medical Image Processing: Techniques and Applications*. Springer, 2011.

[145] Peter Savadjiev, Jaron Chong, Anthony Dohan, Maria Vakalopoulou, Caroline Reinhold, Nikos Paragios, and Benoit Gallix. Demystification of AI-driven medical image interpretation: past, present and future. *European Radiology*, 29(3):1616–1624, 2019.

[146] Paul A. Bromiley, Neil A. Thacker, Marietta L.J. Scott, M. Pokrić, A.J. Lacey, and Timothy F. Cootes. Bayesian and non-Bayesian probabilistic models for medical image analysis. *Image and Vision Computing*, 21(10):851–864, 2003.

[147] Mariano Cabezas, Arnau Oliver, Xavier Lladó, Jordi Freixenet, and Meritxell Bach Cuadra. A review of atlas-based segmentation for magnetic resonance brain images. *Computer Methods and Programs in Biomedicine*, 104(3):e158–e177, 2011.

[148] Pranav Rajpurkar, Jeremy Irvin, Robyn L. Ball, Kaylie Zhu, Brandon Yang, Hershel Mehta, Tony Duan, Daisy Ding, Aarti Bagul, Curtis P. Langlotz, et al. Deep learning for chest radiograph diagnosis: A retrospective comparison of the CheXNeXt algorithm to practicing radiologists. *PLoS Medicine*, 15(11):e1002686, 2018.

[149] William Gale, Luke Oakden-Rayner, Gustavo Carneiro, Andrew P. Bradley, and Lyle J. Palmer. Detecting hip fractures with radiologist-level performance using deep neural networks. *arXiv preprint arXiv:1711.06504*, 2017.

[150] Joseph J. Titano, Marcus Badgeley, Javin Schefflein, Margaret Pain, Andres Su, Michael Cai, Nathaniel Swinburne, John Zech, Jun Kim, Joshua Bederson, et al. Automated deep-neural-network surveillance of cranial images for acute neurologic events. *Nature Medicine*, 24(9):1337–1341, 2018.

[151] Varun Gulshan, Lily Peng, Marc Coram, Martin C. Stumpe, Derek Wu, Arunachalam Narayanaswamy, Subhashini Venugopalan, Kasumi Widner, Tom Madams, Jorge Cuadros, et al. Development and validation of a deep learning algorithm for detection of diabetic retinopathy in retinal fundus photographs. *JAMA*, 316(22):2402–2410, 2016.

[152] Alejandro Rodriguez-Ruiz, Kristina Lång, Albert Gubern-Merida, Jonas Teuwen, Mireille Broeders, Gisella Gennaro, Paola Clauser, Thomas H Helbich, Margarita Chevalier, Thomas Mertelmeier, et al. Can we reduce the workload of mammographic screening by automatic identification of normal exams with artificial intelligence? A feasibility study. *European Radiology*, pages 1–8, 2019.

[153] Alejandro Rodriguez-Ruiz, Kristina Lång, Albert Gubern-Merida, Mireille Broeders, Gisella Gennaro, Paola Clauser, Thomas H. Helbich, Margarita Chevalier, Tao Tan, Thomas Mertelmeier, et al. Stand-alone artificial intelligence for breast cancer detection in mammography: comparison with 101 radiologists. *JNCI: Journal of the National Cancer Institute* 111(9):916–922, 2019.

[154] European Society of Radiology (ESR). What the radiologist should know about artificial intelligence–an ESR white paper. *Insights into Imaging*, 10(1):44, 2019.

[155] The Lancet. Artificial intelligence in health care: within touching distance. *The Lancet*, 390:2739, 2017.

[156] Signify Research. What's new for machine learning in medical imaging -predictions for 2019 and beyond. https://s3-eu-west-2.amazonaws.com/signifyresearch/app/uploads/2018/10/16101114/Signify_AI-in-Medical-Imaging-White-Paper.pdf. Accessed: 2019-07-20.

[157] Concetto Spampinato, Simone Palazzo, Daniela Giordano, Marco Aldinucci, and Rosalia Leonardi. Deep learning for automated skeletal bone age assessment in x-ray images. *Medical Image Analysis*, 36:41–51, 2017.

[158] Gwenolé Quellec, Katia Charrière, Yassine Boudi, Béatrice Cochener, and Mathieu Lamard. Deep image mining for diabetic retinopathy screening. *Medical Image Analysis*, 39:178–193, 2017.

[159] International Skin Imaging Collaboration: Melanoma Project website. available at https://www.isic-archive.com/, 2018.

[160] Eric Scuccimarra. EXTS capstone project. available at https://github.com/escuccim/mias-mammography, 2018. Accessed: 2018-06-01.

[161] Matthew Sinclair, Christian F. Baumgartner, Jacqueline Matthew, Wenjia Bai, Juan Cerrolaza Martinez, Yuanwei Li, Sandra Smith, Caroline L. Knight, Bernhard Kainz, Jo Hajnal, et al. Human-level performance on automatic head biometrics in fetal ultrasound using fully convolutional neural networks. In *2018 40th Annual International Conference of Engineering in Medicine and Biology Society*, IEEE, 2018, pages 714–717.

[162] Rahul Venkataramani, Hariharan Ravishankar, and Saihareesh Anamandra. Towards continuous domain adaptation for medical imaging. In *2019 IEEE 16th International Symposium on Biomedical Imaging (ISBI 2019)*, IEEE, 2019, pages 443–446.

[163] Robert J. Gillies, Paul E. Kinahan, and Hedvig Hricak. Radiomics: images are more than pictures, they are data. *Radiology*, 278(2):563–577, 2015.

[164] Anand Devaraj, Bram van Ginneken, Arjun Nair, and David Baldwin. Use of volumetry for lung nodule management: theory and practice. *Radiology*, 284(3):630–644, 2017.

[165] Filippo Pesapane, Marina Codari, and Francesco Sardanelli. Artificial intelligence in medical imaging: threat or opportunity? Radiologists again at the forefront of innovation in medicine. *European Radiology Experimental*, 2(1):35, 2018.

[166] Habib Zaidi. *Quantitative Analysis in Nuclear Medicine Imaging*. Springer, 2006.

[167] Richard G. Abramson, Kirsteen R. Burton, J. Yu JohnPaul, Ernest M. Scalzetti, Thomas E. Yankeelov, Andrew B. Rosenkrantz, Mishal Mendiratta-Lala, Brian J. Bartholmai, Dhakshinamoorthy Ganeshan, Leon Lenchik, et al. Methods and challenges in quantitative imaging biomarker development. *Academic Radiology*, 22(1):25–32, 2015.

[168] Christian Herz, Jean-Christophe Fillion-Robin, Michael Onken, Jörg Riesmeier, Andras Lasso, Csaba Pinter, Gabor Fichtinger, Steve Pieper, David Clunie, Ron Kikinis, et al. DCMQI: an open source library for standardized communication of quantitative image analysis results using DICOM. *Cancer Research*, 77(21):e87–e90, 2017.

[169] Cindy S. Lee, Paul G. Nagy, Sallie J. Weaver, and David E. Newman-Toker. Cognitive and system factors contributing to diagnostic errors in radiology. *American Journal of Roentgenology*, 201(3):611–617, 2013.

[170] Qiang Li and Robert M. Nishikawa. *Computer-aided Detection and Diagnosis in Medical Imaging*. Taylor & Francis, Boca Raton, FL, 2015.

[171] Oliver Faust, U. Rajendra Acharya, Vidya K. Sudarshan, Ru San Tan, Chai Hong Yeong, Filippo Molinari, and Kwan Hoong Ng. Computer aided diagnosis of coronary artery disease, myocardial infarction and carotid atherosclerosis using ultrasound images: A review. *Physica Medica*, 33:1–15, 2017.

[172] Rangaraj M. Rangayyan, Fabio J. Ayres, and J.E. Leo Desautels. A review of computer-aided diagnosis of breast cancer: Toward the detection of subtle signs. *Journal of the Franklin Institute*, 344(3-4):312–348, 2007.

[173] Guy J. Amir and Harold P. Lehmann. After detection: The improved accuracy of lung cancer assessment using radiologic computer-aided diagnosis. *Academic Radiology*, 23(2):186–191, 2016.

[174] Macedo Firmino, Antônio H Morais, Roberto M. Mendoça, Marcel R. Dantas, Helio R. Hekis, and Ricardo Valentim. Computer-aided detection system for lung cancer in computed tomography scans: review and future prospects. *Biomedical Engineering Online*, 13(1):41, 2014.

[175] Nicholas Petrick, Berkman Sahiner, Samuel Armato III, Alberto Bert, Loredana Correale, Silvia Delsanto, Matthew T Freedman, David Fryd, David Gur, Lubomir Hadjiiski, Zhimin Huo, Yulei Jiang, Lia Morra, Sophie Paquerault, Vikas Raykar, Frank Samuelson, Ronald Summers, Georgia Tourassi, Hiroyuki Yoshida, and Heang-Ping Chan. Evaluation of computer-aided detection and diagnosis systems. *Medical Physics*, 40:087001, 08 2013.

[176] Gabriella Iussich, Loredana Correale, Carlo Senore, Cesare Hassan, Nereo Segnan, Delia Campanella, Alberto Bert, Giovanni Galatola, Cristiana Laudi, and Daniele Regge. Computer-aided detection for computed tomographic colonography screening: a prospective comparison of a double-reading paradigm with first-reader computer-aided detection against second-reader computer-aided detection. *Investigative Radiology*, 49(3):173–182, 2014.

[177] J.B. Antoine Maintz and Max A. Viergever. A survey of medical image registration. *Medical Image Analysis*, 2(1):1–36, 1998.

[178] Valentina Giannini, Anna Vignati, Massimo De Luca, Silvano Agliozzo, Alberto Bert, Lia Morra, Diego Persano, Filippo Molinari, and Daniele Regge. Registration, lesion detection, and discrimination for breast dynamic contrast-enhanced magnetic resonance imaging. In *Multimodality Breast Imaging: Diagnosis and Treatment*, pages 85–112. SPIE, 2013.

[179] Valentina Agostini, Silvia Delsanto, Marco Knaflitz, and Filippo Molinari. Noise estimation in infrared image sequences: a tool for the quantitative evaluation of the effectiveness of registration algorithms. *IEEE Transactions on Biomedical Engineering*, 55(7):1917–1920, 2008.

[180] Joseph V. Hajnal and Derek L.G. Hill. *Medical Image Registration*. CRC Press, Boca Raton, 2001.

[181] Max A Viergever, JB Antoine Maintz, Stefan Klein, Keelin Murphy, Marius Staring, and Josien PW Pluim. A survey of medical image registration–under review. *Medical Image Analysis*, 100(33):140–144, 2016.

[182] Yipeng Hu, Marc Modat, Eli Gibson, Wenqi Li, Nooshin Ghavami, Ester Bonmati, Guotai Wang, Steven Bandula, Caroline M. Moore, Mark Emberton, et al. Weakly-supervised convolutional neural networks for multimodal image registration. *Medical Image Analysis*, 49:1–13, 2018.

[183] Hongming Li and Yong Fan. Non-rigid image registration using fully convolutional networks with deep self-supervision. *arXiv preprint arXiv:1709.00799*, 2017.

[184] Philippe Lambin, Emmanuel Rios-Velazquez, Ralph Leije-naar, Sara Carvalho, Ruud G.P.M. Van Stiphout, Patrick Granton, Catharina M.L. Zegers, Robert Gillies, Ronald Boellard, André Dekker, et al. Radiomics: extracting more information from medical images using advanced feature analysis. *European Journal of Cancer*, 48(4):441–446, 2012.

[185] Alberto Traverso, Leonard Wee, Andre Dekker, and Robert Gillies. Repeatability and reproducibility of radiomic features: a systematic review. *International Journal of Radiation Oncology* Biology* Physics*, 102(4):1143–1158, 2018.

[186] Mu Zhou, Jacob Scott, Baishali Chaudhury, Lawrence Hall, Dmitry Goldof, Kristen W. Yeom, Michael Iv, Yangming Ou, Jayashree Kalpathy-Cramer, Sandy Napel, et al. Radiomics in brain tumor: image assessment, quantitative feature descriptors, and machine-learning approaches. *American Journal of Neuroradiology*, 39(2):208–216, 2018.

[187] Michael D. Kuo, Jeremy Gollub, Claude B. Sirlin, Clara Ooi, and Xin Chen. Radiogenomic analysis to identify imaging phenotypes associated with drug response gene expression programs in hepatocellular carcinoma. *Journal of Vascular and Interventional Radiology*, 18(7):821–830, 2007.

[188] Philippe Lambin, Ralph T.H. Leijenaar, Timo M. Deist, Jurgen Peerlings, Evelyn E.C. De Jong, Janita Van Timmeren, Sebastian Sanduleanu, Ruben T.H.M. Larue, Aniek J.G. Even, Arthur Jochems, et al. Radiomics: the bridge between medical imaging and personalized medicine. *Nature Reviews Clinical Oncology*, 14(12):749, 2017.

[189] Christos Davatzikos, Saima Rathore, Spyridon Bakas, Sarthak Pati, Mark Bergman, Ratheesh Kalarot, Patmaa Sridharan, Aimilia Gastounioti, Nariman Jahani, Eric Cohen, et al. Cancer imaging phenomics toolkit: quantitative imaging analytics for precision diagnostics and predictive modeling of clinical outcome. *Journal of Medical Imaging*, 5(1):011018, 2018.

[190] Paras Lakhani, Adam B. Prater, R. Kent Hutson, Kathy P. Andriole, Keith J. Dreyer, Jose Morey, Luciano M. Prevedello, Toshi J. Clark, J. Raymond Geis, Jason N. Itri, et al. Machine learning in radiology: applications beyond image interpretation. *Journal of the American College of Radiology*, 15(2):350–359, 2018.

[191] Zhongyu Li, Xiaofan Zhang, Henning Müller, and Shaoting Zhang. Large-scale retrieval for medical image analytics: A comprehensive review. *Medical Image Analysis*, 43:66–84, 2018.

[192] Metin N. Gurcan, Laura Boucheron, Ali Can, Anant Madabhushi, Nasir Rajpoot, and Bulent Yener. Histopathological image analysis: A review. *IEEE Reviews in Biomedical Engineering*, 2:147, 2009.

[193] Daisuke Komura and Shumpei Ishikawa. Machine learning methods for histopathological image analysis. *Computational and Structural Biotechnology Journal*, 16:34–42, 2018.

[194] Maylene Wong, Josef Edelstein, Jerome Wollman, and M. Gene Bond. Ultrasonic-pathological comparison of the human arterial wall. verification of intima-media thickness. *Arteriosclerosis and Thrombosis: A Journal of Vascular Biology*, 13(4):482–486, 1993.

[195] I. Wendelhag, T. Gustavsson, M. Suurküla, G. Berglund, and J. Wikstrand. Ultrasound measurement of wall thickness in the carotid artery: fundamental principles and description of a computerized analysing system. *Clinical Physiology*, 11(6):565–577, 1991.

[196] Inger Wendelhag, Quan Liang, Tomas Gustavsson, and John Wikstrand. A new automated computerized analyzing system simplifies readings and reduces the variability in ultrasound measurement of intima-media thickness. *Stroke*, 28(11):2195–2200, 1997.

[197] Consolatina Liguori, Alfredo Paolillo, and Antonio Pietrosanto. An automatic measurement system for the evaluation of carotid intima-media thickness. *IEEE Transactions on Instrumentation and Measurement*, 50(6):1684–1691, 2001.

[198] Marco A. Gutierrez, Paulo E. Pilon, S.G. Lage, L. Kopel, R.T. Carvalho, and S.S. Furuie. Automatic measurement of carotid diameter and wall thickness in ultrasound images. In *Computers in Cardiology*, pages 359–362. IEEE, 2002.

[199] Silvia Delsanto, Filippo Molinari, Pierangela Giustetto, William Liboni, Sergio Badalamenti, and Jasjit S Suri. Characterization of a completely user-independent algorithm for carotid artery segmentation in 2-D ultrasound images. *IEEE Transactions on Instrumentation and Measurement*, 56(4):1265–1274, 2007.

[200] Alberto Bert, Ivan Dmitriev, Silvano Agliozzo, Natalia Pietrosemoli, Mark Mandelkern, Teresa Gallo, and Daniele Regge. An automatic method for colon segmentation in CT colonography. *Computerized Medical Imaging and Graphics*, 33(4):325–331, 2009.

[201] A. Kronman, Leo Joskowicz, and Jacob Sosna. Anatomical structures segmentation by spherical 3D ray casting and gradient domain editing. In *International Conference on Medical Image Computing and Computer-Assisted Intervention*, pages 363–370. Springer, Berlin, Heidelberg, 2012.

[202] Mainak Biswas, Venkatanareshbabu Kuppili, Tadashi Araki, Damodar Reddy Edla, Elisa Cuadrado Godia, Luca Saba, Harman S. Suri, Tomaž Omerzu, John R. Laird, Narendra N. Khanna, et al. Deep learning strategy for accurate carotid intima-media thickness measurement: an ultrasound study on Japanese diabetic cohort. *Computers in Biology and Medicine*, 98:100–117, 2018.

[203] Silvia Delsanto, Lia Morra, Silvano Agliozzo, Riccardo Baggio, Delia Campanella, Vincenzo Tartaglia, Francesca Cerri, Franco Iafrate, Emanuele Neri, Andrea Laghi, et al. Computer aided detection of polyps in virtual colonoscopy with sameday faecal tagging. In *Medical Imaging 2008: Computer-Aided Diagnosis*, volume 6915, 2008.

[204] Lia Morra, Silvia Delsanto, and Giulia Grazzini. *Computer-Aided Diagnosis for X-ray Imaging, in Handbook of X-ray Imaging: Physics and Technology*, pages 1211–1226. CRC Press, 2017.

[205] Hiroyuki Yoshida, Janne Näppi, Peter MacEneaney, David T. Rubin, and Abraham H. Dachman. Computer-aided diagnosis scheme for detection of polyps at CT colonography. *Radiographics*, 22(4):963–979, 2002.

[206] Rie Tachibana, Janne J. Näppi, Toru Hironakaa, Se Hyung Kim, and Hiroyuki Yoshida. Deep learning for electronic cleansing in dual-energy CT colonography. In *Medical Imaging 2016: Computer-Aided Diagnosis*, volume 9785, page 97851M. International Society for Optics and Photonics, 2016.

[207] Janne J. Näppi, Toru Hironaka, Daniele Regge, and Hiroyuki Yoshida. Deep transfer learning of virtual endoluminal views for the detection of polyps in CT colonography. In *Medical Imaging 2016: Computer-Aided Diagnosis*, volume 9785, page 97852B, 2016.

[208] I. Reiser and I. Sechopoulos. A review of digital breast tomosynthesis. *Medical Physics International Journal*, 2014.

[209] R. Chersevani, S. Ciatto, C. Del Favero, A. Frigerio, L. Giordano, G. Giuseppetti, C. Naldoni, P. Panizza, M. Petrella, and G. Saguatti. "CADEAT": considerations on the use of CAD (computer-aided diagnosis) in mammography. *La Radiologia Medica*, 115(4):563–570, 2010.

[210] Constance D. Lehman, Robert D. Wellman, Diana S.M. Buist, Karla Kerlikowske, Anna N.A. Tosteson, and Diana L. Miglioretti. Diagnostic accuracy of digital screening mammography with and without computer-aided detection. *JAMA Internal Medicine*, 175(11):1828–1837, 2015.

[211] Arnau Oliver, Jordi Freixenet, Joan Marti, Elsa Perez, Josep Pont, Erika R.E. Denton, and Reyer Zwiggelaar. A review of automatic mass detection and segmentation in mammographic images. *Medical Image Analysis*, 14(2):87–110, 2010.

[212] Heang-Ping Chan, Jun Wei, Yiheng Zhang, Mark A. Helvie, Richard H. Moore, Berkman Sahiner, Lubomir Hadjiiski, and Daniel B. Kopans. Computer-aided detection of masses in digital tomosynthesis mammography: Comparison of three approaches. *Medical Physics*, 35(9):4087–4095, 2008.

[213] Berkman Sahiner, Heang-Ping Chan, Nicholas Petrick, Mark A. Helvie, and Lubomir M. Hadjiiski. Improvement of mammographic mass characterization using spiculation measures and morphological features. *Medical Physics*, 28(7): 1455–1465, 2001.

[214] Hrishikesh Haldankar, Jeffrey W. Hoffmeister, Senthil Peri-aswamy, Sergei V. Fotin, and Yin Yin. Detection of soft tissue densities from digital breast tomosynthesis: Comparison of conventional and deep learning approaches. In *Proceedings of Medical Imaging 2016: Computer-Aided Diagnosis*, vol. 9785, p. 97850X. International Society for Optics and Photonics, 2016.

[215] Thijs Kooi, Geert Litjens, Bram van Ginneken, Albert Gubern-Mérida, Clara I. Sánchez, Ritse Mann, Ard den Heeten, and Nico Karssemeijer. Large scale deep learning for computer aided detection of mammographic lesions. *Medical Image Analysis*, 35:303–312, 2017.

[216] Neeraj Dhungel, Gustavo Carneiro, and Andrew P. Bradley. The automated learning of deep features for breast mass classification from mammograms. In *International Conference on Medical Image Computing and Computer-Assisted Intervention*, pages 106–114. Springer, 2016.

[217] Ravi Samala, Heang-Ping Chan, Lubomir Hadjiiski, Mark A Helvie, Jun Wei, and Kenny Cha. Mass detection in digital breast tomosynthesis: Deep convolutional neural network with transfer learning from mammography. *Medical Physics*, 43:6654, 12 2016.

[218] Mohammed Al-masni, Mugahed A. Al-antari, Jeong-min Park, Geon Gi, Tae-Yeon Kim, Patricio Rivera, Edwin Valarezo, Mun-Taek Choi, Seung-Moo Han, and Tae-Seong Kim. Simultaneous detection and classification of breast masses in digital mammograms via a deep learning YOLO-based CAD system. *Computer Methods and Programs in Biomedicine*, 157(2018):85–94.

[219] Nan Wu, Jason Phang, Jungkyu Park, Yiqiu Shen, Zhe Huang, Masha Zorin, Stanisław Jastrzębski, Thibault Févry, Joe Katsnelson, Eric Kim, et al. Deep neural networks improve radiologists' performance in breast cancer screening. *arXiv preprint arXiv:1903.08297*, 2019.

[220] William Lotter, Greg Sorensen, and David Cox. A multiscale CNN and curriculum learning strategy for mammogram classification. *CoRR*, abs/1707.06978, 2017.

[221] Thijs Kooi, Jan-Jurre Mordang, and Nico Karssemeijer. Conditional random field modelling of interactions between findings in mammography. In *Medical Imaging 2017: Computer-Aided Diagnosis*, volume 10134, page 101341E, 2017.

[222] Thijs Kooi and Nico Karssemeijer. Classifying symmetrical differences and temporal change for the detection of malignant masses in mammography using deep neural networks. *Journal of Medical Imaging*, 4(4):044501, 2017.

[223] Wentao Zhu, Qi Lou, Yeeleng Scott Vang, and Xiaohui Xie. Deep multi-instance networks with sparse label assignment for whole mammogram classification. *CoRR*, abs/1612.05968, 2016.

[224] Darvin Yi, Rebecca Lynn Sawyer, David Cohn III, Jared Dunnmon, Carson Lam, Xuerong Xiao, and Daniel L. Rubin. Optimizing and visualizing deep learning for benign/malignant classification in breast tumors. *arXiv preprint arXiv:1705.06362*, 2017.

[225] Jan-Jurre Mordang, Tim Janssen, Alessandro Bria, Thijs Kooi, Albert Gubern-Mérida, and Nico Karssemeijer. Automatic microcalcification detection in multi-vendor mammography using convolutional neural networks. In *International Workshop on Digital Mammography*, pages 35–42. Springer, 2016.

[226] Jinhua Wang, Xi Yang, Hongmin Cai, Wanchang Tan, Cangzheng Jin, and Li Li. Discrimination of breast cancer with microcalcifications on mammography by deep learning. *Scientific Reports*, 6:27327, 2016.

[227] Benjamin Q. Huynh, Hui Li, and Maryellen L. Giger. Digital mammographic tumor classification using transfer learning from deep convolutional neural networks. *Journal of Medical Imaging*, 3 3:034501, 2016.

[228] Seema Garg and Richard M. Davis. Diabetic retinopathy screening update. *Clinical Diabetes*, 27(4):140–145, 2009.

[229] Diabetes. https://www.who.int/news-room/fact-sheets/detail/diabetes. Accessed: 2019-07-27.

[230] Varun Gulshan, Renu P. Rajan, Kasumi Widner, Derek Wu, Peter Wubbels, Tyler Rhodes, Kira Whitehouse, Marc Coram, Greg Corrado, Kim Ramasamy, et al. Performance of a deep-learning algorithm vs manual grading for detecting diabetic retinopathy in India. *JAMA Ophthalmology*, 2019.

[231] Ryan Poplin, Avinash V. Varadarajan, Katy Blumer, Yun Liu, Michael V. McConnell, Greg S. Corrado, Lily Peng, and Dale R. Webster. Prediction of cardiovascular risk factors from retinal fundus photographs via deep learning. *Nature Biomedical Engineering*, 2(3):158, 2018.

[232] Ramachandran Rajalakshmi, Radhakrishnan Subashini, Ranjit Mohan Anjana, and Viswanathan Mohan. Automated diabetic retinopathy detection in smartphone-based fundus photography using artificial intelligence. *Eye*, 32(6):1138, 2018.

[233] Jonathan Krause, Varun Gulshan, Ehsan Rahimy, Peter Karth, Kasumi Widner, Greg S. Corrado, Lily Peng, and Dale R. Webster. Grader variability and the importance of reference standards for evaluating machine learning models for diabetic retinopathy. *Ophthalmology*, 125(8):1264–1272, 2018.

[234] Software as a Medical Device Working Group. Software as a medical device (SaMD): Clinical evaluation. http://www.imdrf.org/docs/imdrf/final/technical/imdrf-tech-170921-samd-n41-clinical-evaluation_1.pdf. Accessed: 2019-07-28.

[235] Zhimin Huo, Ronald M. Summers, Sophie Paquerault, Joseph Lo, Jeffrey Hoffmeister, Samuel G. Armato III, Matthew T. Freedman, Jesse Lin, Shih-Chung Ben Lo, Nicholas Petrick, et al. Quality assurance and training procedures for computer-aided detection and diagnosis systems in clinical use. *Medical Physics*, 40(7):077001, 2013.

[236] Delia Campanella, Lia Morra, Silvia Delsanto, Vincenzo Tartaglia, Roberto Asnaghi, Alberto Bert, Emanuele Neri, and Daniele Regge. Comparison of three different iodine-based bowel regimens for CT colonography. *European Radiology*, 20(2):348–358, 2010.

[237] Emanuele Neri, Philippe Lefere, Stefaan Gryspeerdt, Pietro Bemi, Annalisa Mantarro, and Carlo Bartolozzi. Bowel preparation for CT colonography. *European Journal of Radiology*, 82(8):1137–1143, 2013.

[238] E. Keavey, N. Phelan, A.M. O'Connell, F. Flanagan, A. O'Doherty, A. Larke, and A.M. Connors. Comparison of the clinical performance of three digital mammography systems in a breast cancer screening programme. *British Journal of Radiology*, 85(1016):1123–1127, 2012.

[239] Ravi K. Samala, Heang-Ping Chan, Yao Lu, Lubomir M. Hadjiiski, Jun Wei, and Mark A. Helvie. Digital breast tomosynthesis: computer-aided detection of clustered microcalcifications on planar projection images. *Physics Medical Biology*, 59(29):7457–7477, 2014.

[240] P. Lo, S. Young, H. J. Kim, M. S. Brown, and M. F. McNitt-Gray. Variability in CT lung-nodule quantification: Effects of dose reduction and reconstruction methods on density and texture based features. *Medical Physics*, 43(8):4854, 2016.

[241] Faisal Mahmood, Richard Chen, and Nicholas J. Durr. Polyp miss rate determined by tandem colonoscopy: A systematic review. *American Journal of Gastroenterology*, 101:43–50, 2006.

[242] Xin He and Eric Frey. ROC, LROC, FROC, AFROC: An alphabet soup. *Journal of the American College of Radiology*, 6(9):652–655, 2009.

[243] Junji Shiraishi, Lorenzo L. Pesce, Charles E. Metz, and Kunio Doi. Experimental design and data analysis in receiver operating characteristic studies: Lessons learned from reports in radiology from 1997 to 2006. *Radiology*, 253(3):822–830, 2009.

[244] David L. Raunig, Lisa M. McShane, Gene Pennello, Constantine Gatsonis, Paul L. Carson, James T. Voyvodic, Richard L. Wahl, Brenda F. Kurland, Adam J. Schwarz, Mithat Gönen, et al. Quantitative imaging biomarkers: a review of statistical methods for technical performance assessment. *Statistical Methods in Medical Research*, 24(1):27–67, 2015.

[245] Ji Eun Park, Seo Young Park, Hwa Jung Kim, and Ho Sung Kim. Reproducibility and generalizability in radiomics modeling: Possible strategies in radiologic and statistical perspectives. *Korean Journal of Radiology*, 20(7):1124–1137, 2019.

[246] European Society of Radiology (ESR). Magnetic Resonance Fingerprinting - a promising new approach to obtain standardized imaging biomarkers from MRI. *Insights into Imaging*, 6(2):163–165, 2015.

[247] Andrew J. Buckler, Linda Bresolin, N. Reed Dunnick, Daniel C. Sullivan, and Group. A collaborative enterprise for multi-stakeholder participation in the advancement of quantitative imaging. *Radiology*, 258(3):906–914, 2011.

[248] Food and Drug Administration. Proposed regulatory framework for modifications to artificial intelligence/machine learning-based software as a medical device. https://www.fda.gov/media/122535/download.

[249] Nehmat Houssami, Georgia Kirkpatrick-Jones, Naomi Noguchi, and Christoph Lee. Artificial intelligence (AI) for the early detection of breast cancer: a scoping review to assess AI's potential in breast screening practice. *Expert Review of Medical Devices*, 16, 04 2019.

[250] US Food and Drug Administration website. https://www.accessdata.fda.gov/cdrh_docs/pdf16/k163253.pdf. Accessed: 2019-03-30.

[251] US Food and Drug Administration website. https://www.accessdata.fda.gov/scripts/cdrh/cfdocs/cfpma/pma_template.cfm?id=p150043. Accessed: 2019-03-30.

[252] Seong Ho Park and Kyunghwa Han. Methodologic guide for evaluating clinical performance and effect of artificial intelligence technology for medical diagnosis and prediction. *Radiology*, 286(3):800–809, 2018.

[253] Daniele Regge, Gabriella Iussich, Nereo Segnan, Loredana Correale, Cesare Hassan, Arrigo Arrigoni, Roberto Asnaghi, Piero Bestagini, Gianmarco Bulighin, Maria Carla Cassinis, et al. Comparing CT colonography and flexible sigmoidoscopy: a randomised trial within a population-based screening programme. *Gut*, 66(8):1434–1440, 2017.

[254] John Concato, Nirav Shah, and Ralph Horwitz. *Randomized, Controlled Trials, Observational Studies, and the Hierarchy of Research Designs*, pages 207–212, 2017.

[255] AI versus MD. What happens when diagnosis is automated? https://www.newyorker.com/magazine/2017/04/03/ai-versus-md. Accessed: 2019-07-30.

[256] Eric Topol. *Deep Medicine: How Artificial Intelligence Can Make Healthcare Human Again*. Hachette, UK, 2019.

[257] Luke Hutton and Tristan Henderson. Beyond the EULA: Improving consent for data mining. In *Transparent Data Mining for Big and Small Data*, pages 147–167. Springer, 2017.

[258] How health care data and lax rules help China prosper in AI. https://www.wired.com/story/health-care-data-lax-rules-help-china-prosper-ai/. Accessed: 2019-07-30.

[259] US and Chinese companies race to dominate AI. https://www.wsj.com/articles/why-u-s-companies-may-lose-the-ai-race-1516280677. Accessed: 2019-07-30.

[260] European Society of Radiology (ESR). ESR position paper on imaging biobanks. *Insights into Imaging*, 6(4):403–410, 2015.

[261] Emanuele Neri and Daniele Regge. Imaging biobanks in oncology: European perspective. *Future Oncology*, 13(5):433–441, 2017.

[262] Adam Yala, Constance Lehman, Tal Schuster, Tally Portnoi, and Regina Barzilay. A deep learning mammography-based model for improved breast cancer risk prediction. *Radiology*, page 182716, 2019.

[263] Andreas Holzinger, Chris Biemann, Constantinos S. Pattichis, and Douglas B. Kell. What do we need to build explainable AI systems for the medical domain? *arXiv preprint arXiv:1712.09923*, 2017.

[264] Derek Doran, Sarah Schulz, and Tarek R. Besold. What does explainable AI really mean? A new conceptualization of perspectives. CEUR *Workshop Proceedings*, vol. 2071, 2018.

Index

Printed in the United States
by Baker & Taylor Publisher Services